A Valentine for
Charlie Brown

Vale

for Char

ntine

e Brown

by Charles M. Schulz

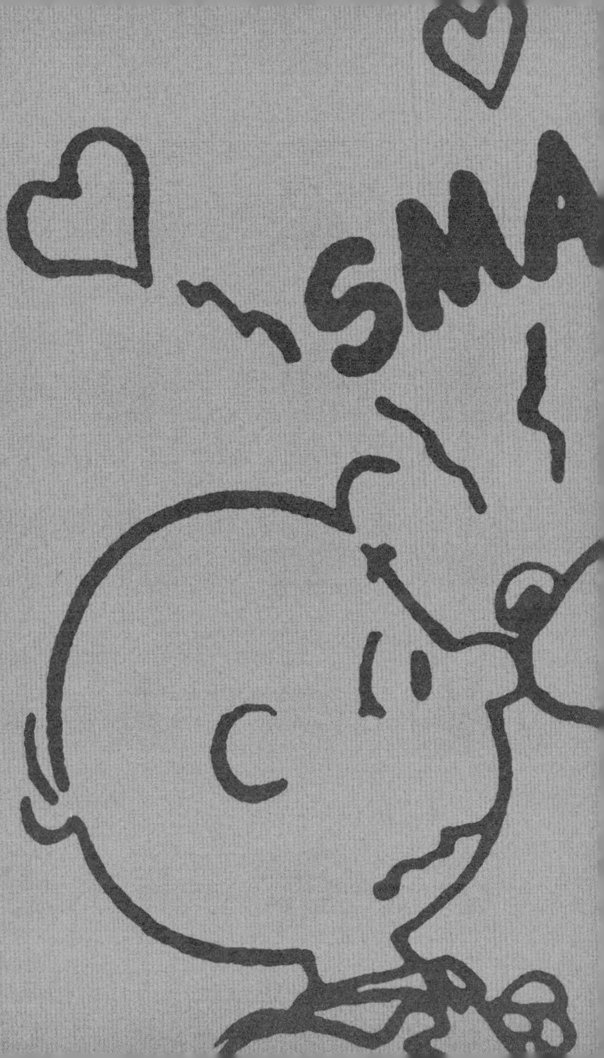
SMA

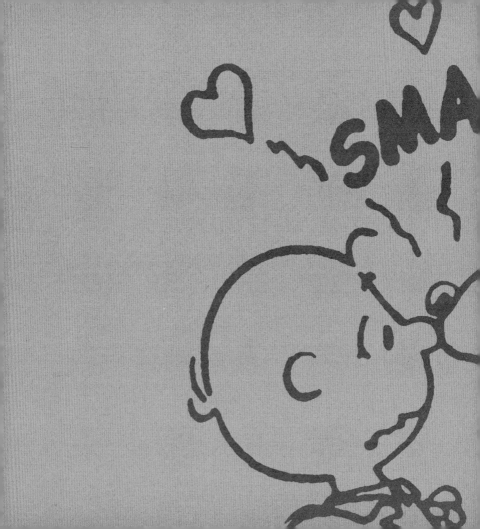

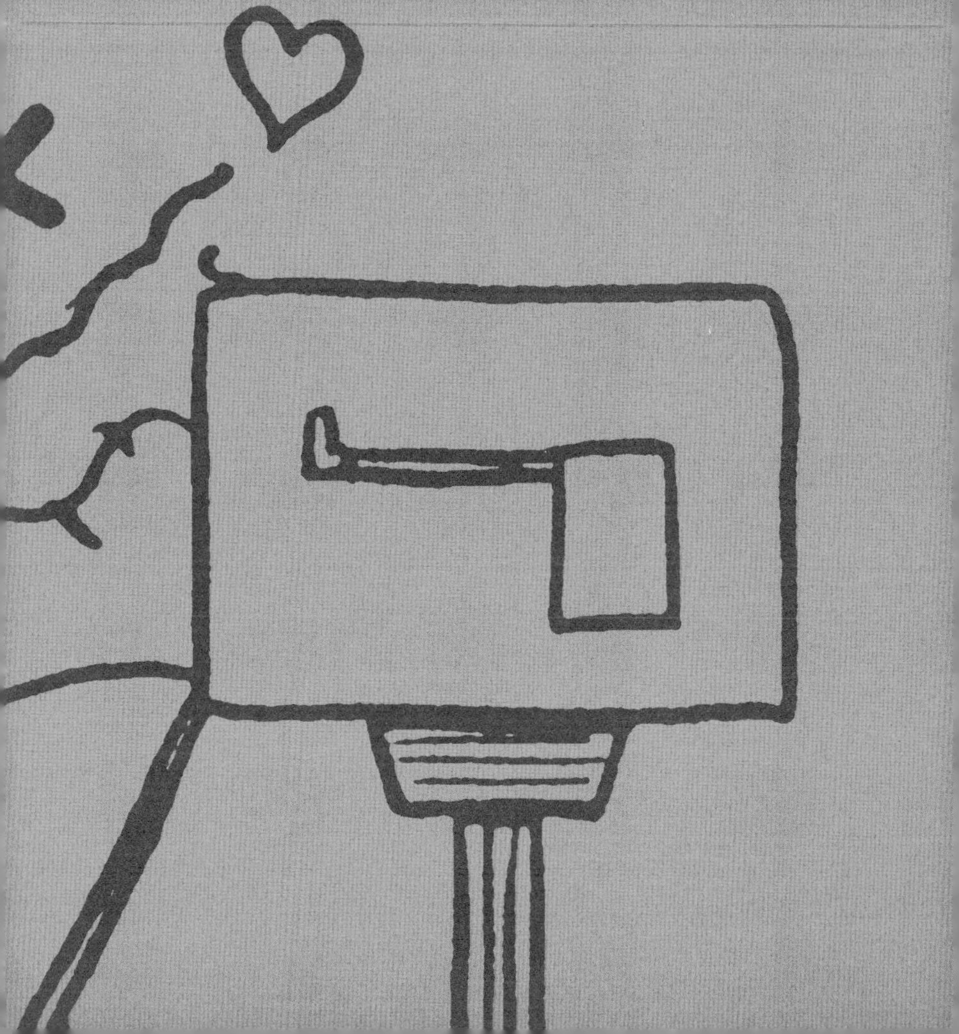

Contents

Valentine's Vigil at the Mailbox

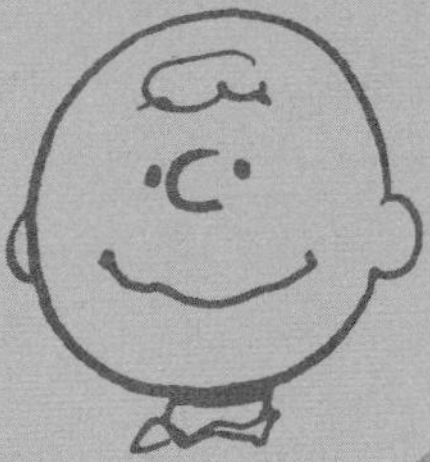

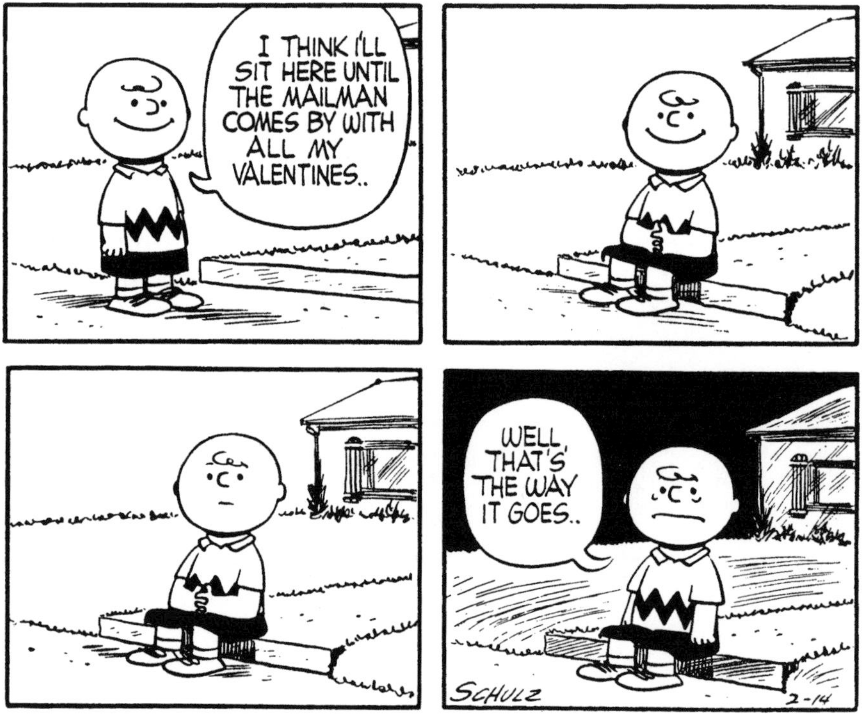
I THINK I'LL SIT HERE UNTIL THE MAILMAN COMES BY WITH ALL MY VALENTINES..
WELL, THAT'S THE WAY IT GOES..
SCHULZ
2-14

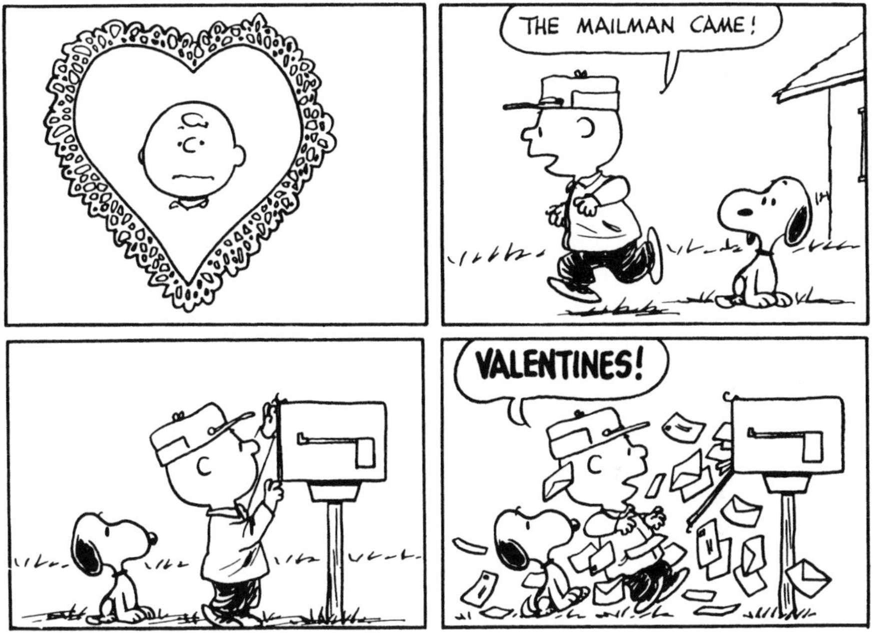
THE MAILMAN CAME!
VALENTINES!

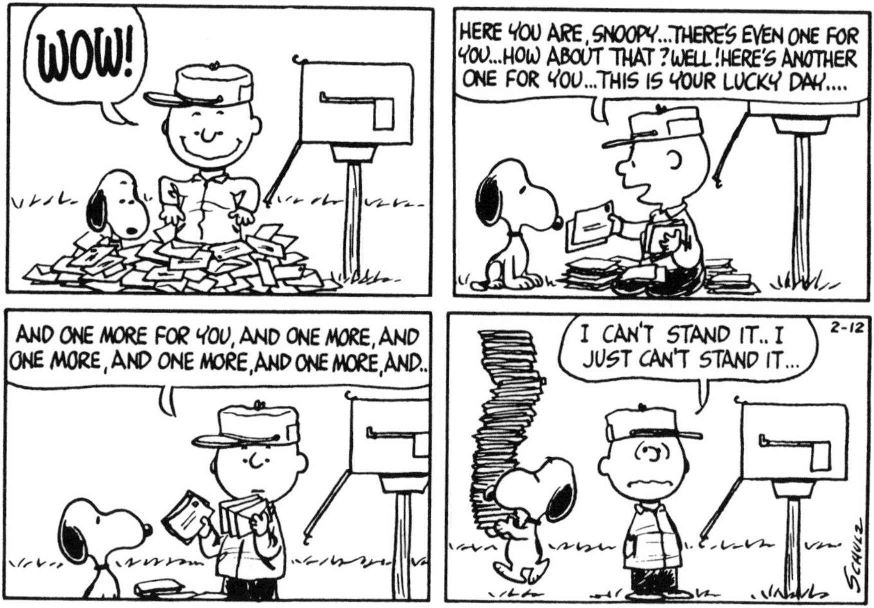
WOW!
HERE YOU ARE, SNOOPY...THERE'S EVEN ONE FOR YOU...HOW ABOUT THAT? WELL! HERE'S ANOTHER ONE FOR YOU...THIS IS YOUR LUCKY DAY....
AND ONE MORE FOR YOU, AND ONE MORE, AND ONE MORE, AND ONE MORE, AND ONE MORE, AND..
2-12
I CAN'T STAND IT.. I JUST CAN'T STAND IT...
SCHULZ

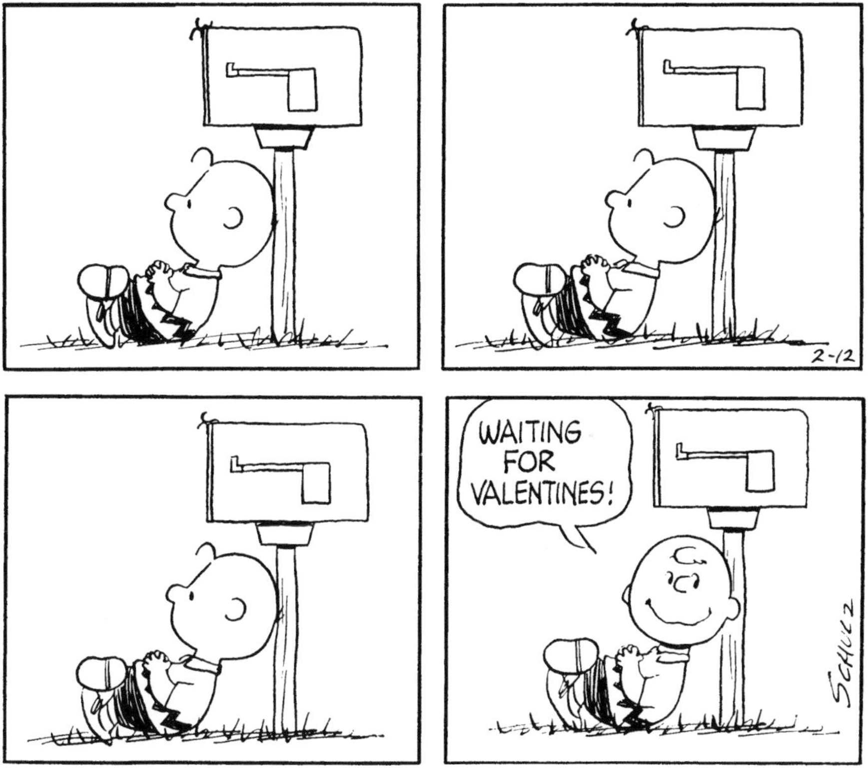
2-12
WAITING FOR VALENTINES!
SCHULZ

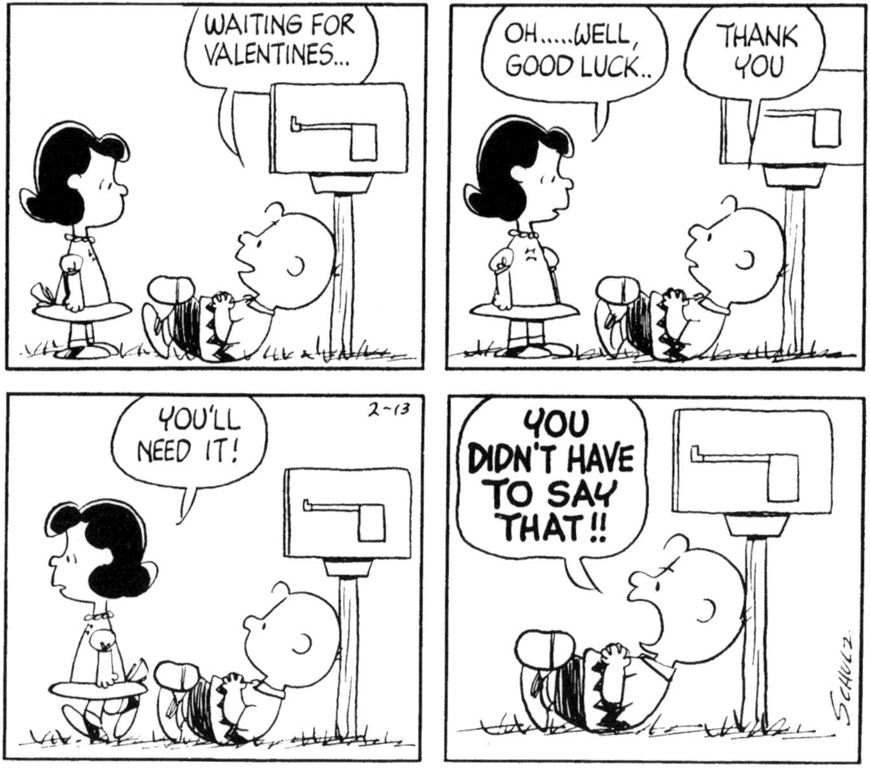
WAITING FOR VALENTINES...
OH.....WELL, GOOD LUCK..
THANK YOU
YOU'LL NEED IT!
2-13
YOU DIDN'T HAVE TO SAY THAT!!
SCHULZ

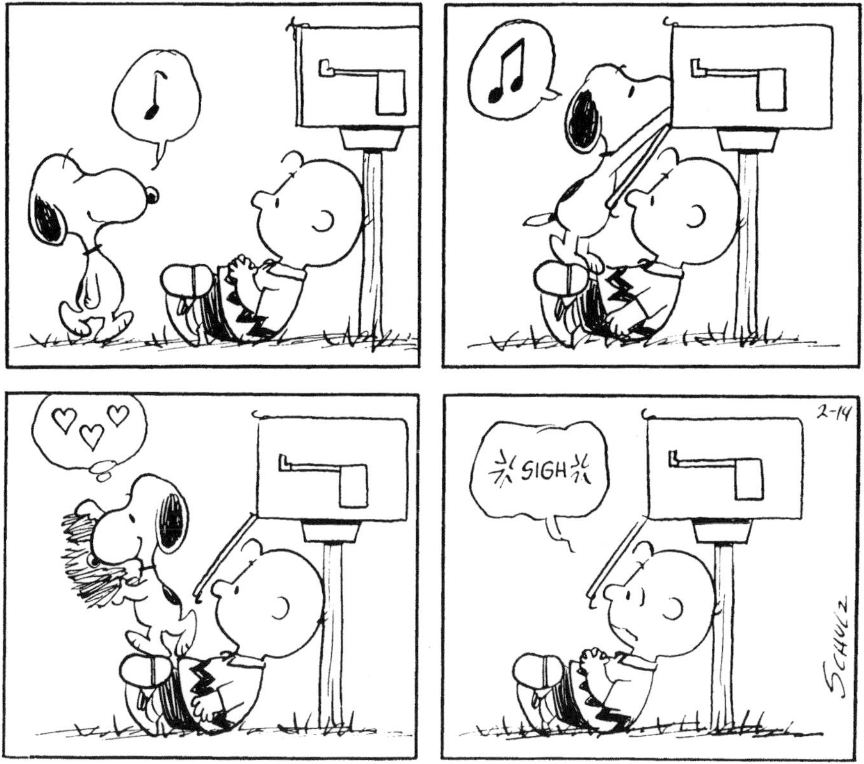
2-14
SIGH
SCHULZ

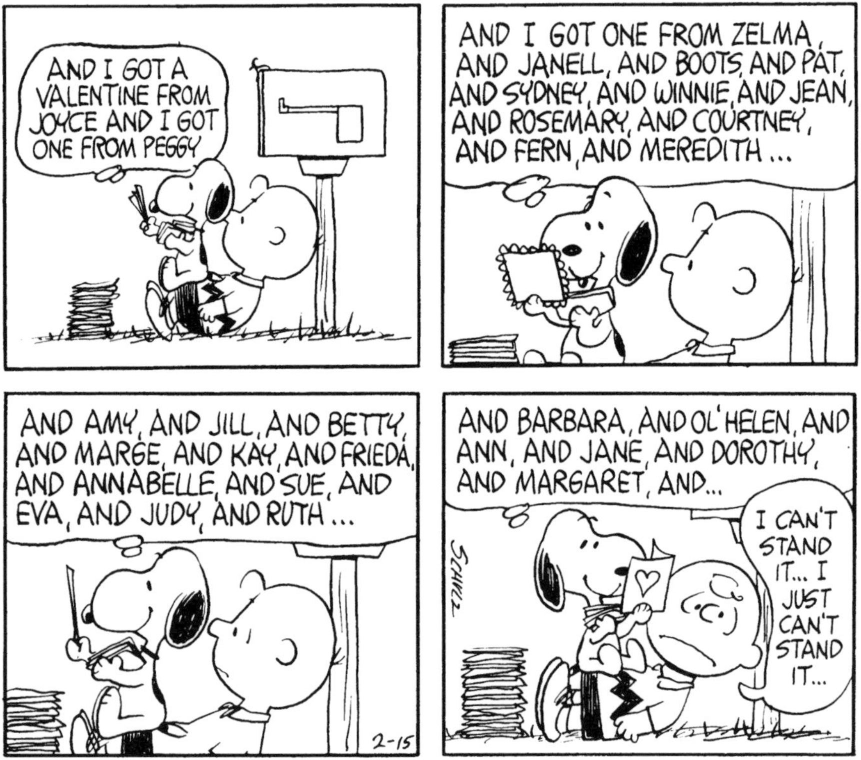
AND I GOT A VALENTINE FROM JOYCE AND I GOT ONE FROM PEGGY
AND I GOT ONE FROM ZELMA, AND JANELL, AND BOOTS, AND PAT, AND SYDNEY, AND WINNIE, AND JEAN, AND ROSEMARY, AND COURTNEY, AND FERN, AND MEREDITH ...
AND AMY, AND JILL, AND BETTY, AND MARGE, AND KAY, AND FRIEDA, AND ANNABELLE, AND SUE, AND EVA, AND JUDY, AND RUTH ...
2-15
AND BARBARA, AND OL' HELEN, AND ANN, AND JANE, AND DOROTHY, AND MARGARET, AND...
SCHULZ
I CAN'T STAND IT... I JUST CAN'T STAND IT...

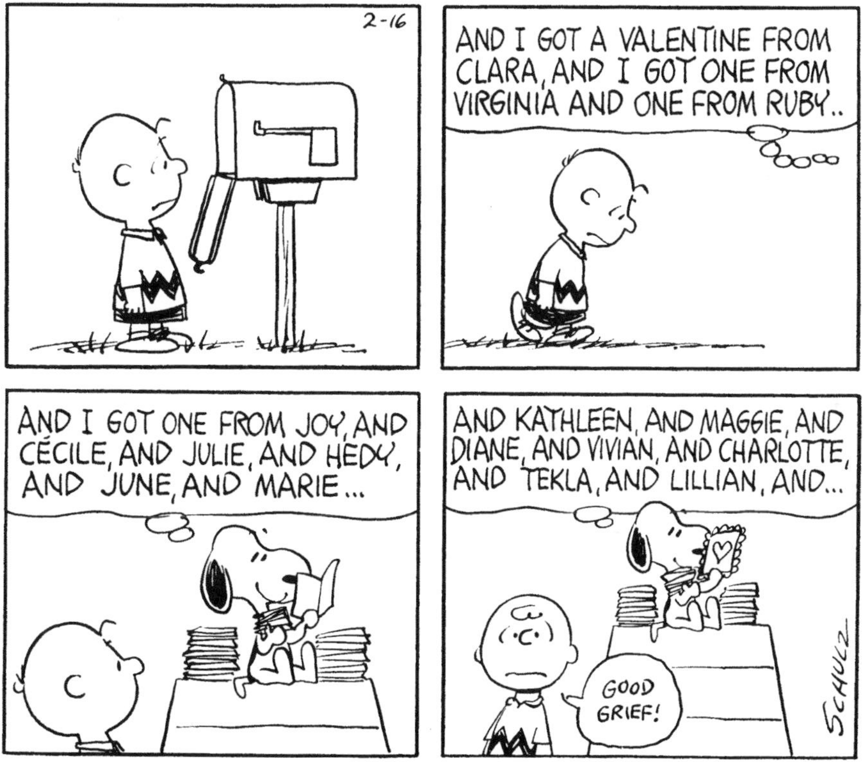
2-16
AND I GOT A VALENTINE FROM CLARA, AND I GOT ONE FROM VIRGINIA AND ONE FROM RUBY..
AND I GOT ONE FROM JOY, AND CÉCILE, AND JULIE, AND HEDY, AND JUNE, AND MARIE...
AND KATHLEEN, AND MAGGIE, AND DIANE, AND VIVIAN, AND CHARLOTTE, AND TEKLA, AND LILLIAN, AND...
GOOD GRIEF!
SCHULZ

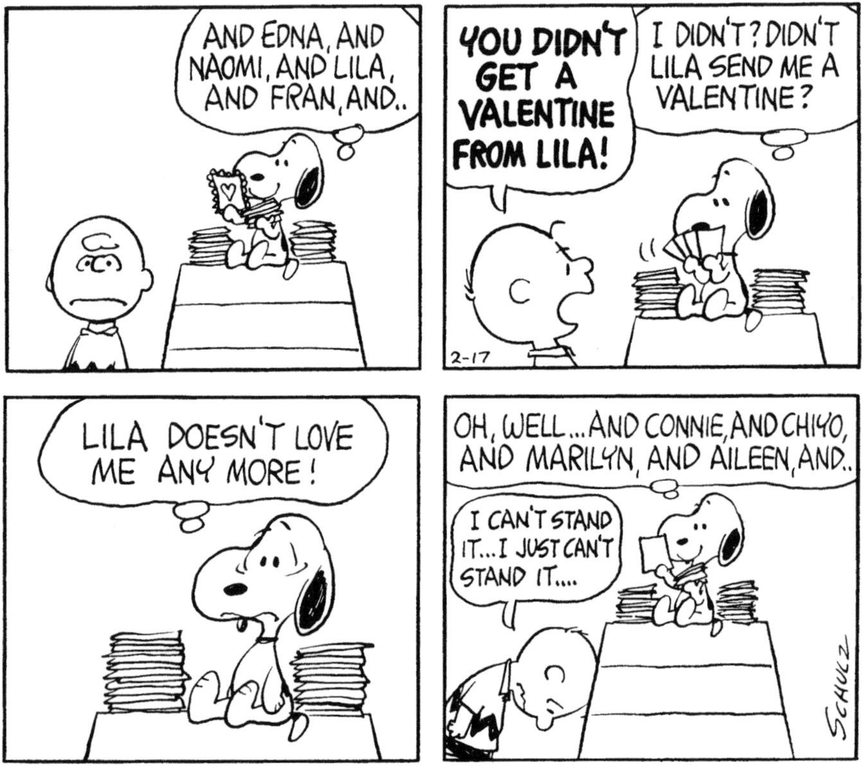
AND EDNA, AND NAOMI, AND LILA, AND FRAN, AND..
YOU DIDN'T GET A VALENTINE FROM LILA!
I DIDN'T? DIDN'T LILA SEND ME A VALENTINE?
2-17
LILA DOESN'T LOVE ME ANY MORE!
OH, WELL... AND CONNIE, AND CHIYO, AND MARILYN, AND AILEEN, AND..
I CAN'T STAND IT... I JUST CAN'T STAND IT....
SCHULZ

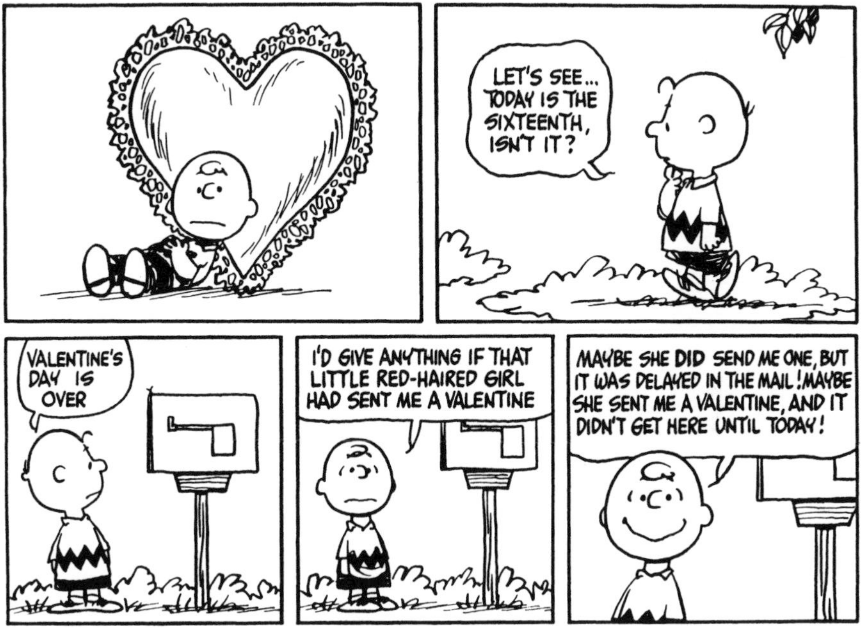
LET'S SEE... TODAY IS THE SIXTEENTH, ISN'T IT?
VALENTINE'S DAY IS OVER
I'D GIVE ANYTHING IF THAT LITTLE RED-HAIRED GIRL HAD SENT ME A VALENTINE
MAYBE SHE **DID** SEND ME ONE, BUT IT WAS DELAYED IN THE MAIL! MAYBE SHE SENT ME A VALENTINE, AND IT DIDN'T GET HERE UNTIL TODAY!

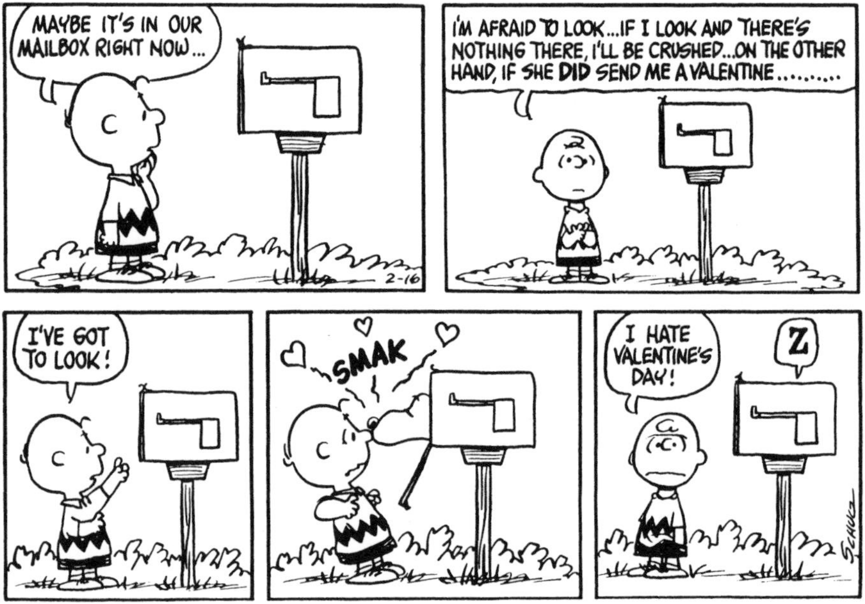
MAYBE IT'S IN OUR MAILBOX RIGHT NOW...
2-16
I'M AFRAID TO LOOK...IF I LOOK AND THERE'S NOTHING THERE, I'LL BE CRUSHED...ON THE OTHER HAND, IF SHE **DID** SEND ME A VALENTINE.........
I'VE GOT TO LOOK!
SMAK
I HATE VALENTINE'S DAY!
Z
SCHULZ

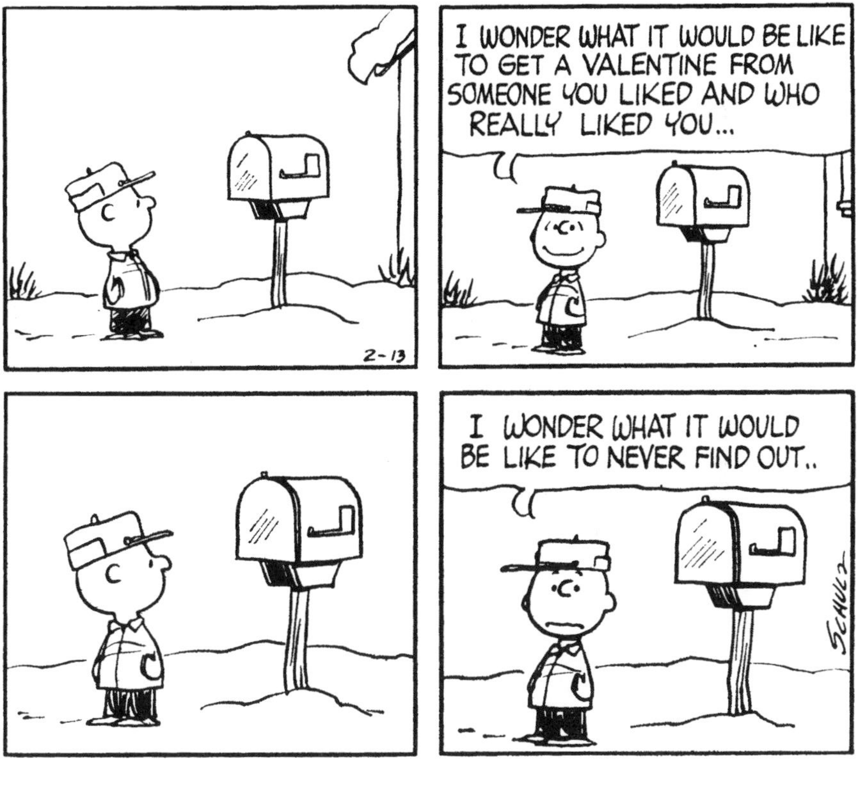
2-13
I WONDER WHAT IT WOULD BE LIKE TO GET A VALENTINE FROM SOMEONE YOU LIKED AND WHO REALLY LIKED YOU...
I WONDER WHAT IT WOULD BE LIKE TO NEVER FIND OUT..
SCHULZ

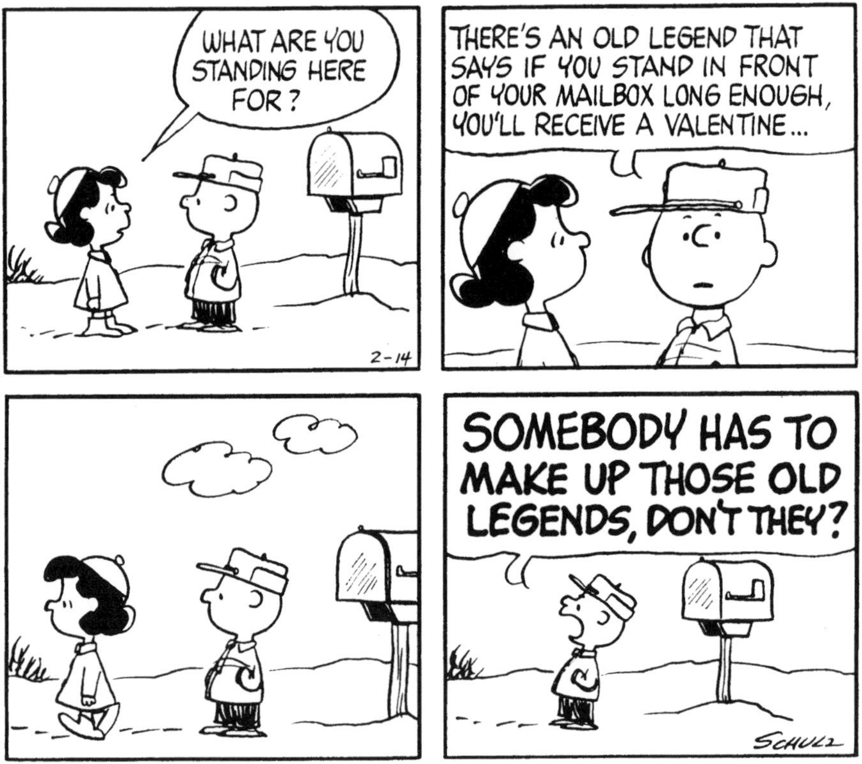
WHAT ARE YOU STANDING HERE FOR?
2-14
THERE'S AN OLD LEGEND THAT SAYS IF YOU STAND IN FRONT OF YOUR MAILBOX LONG ENOUGH, YOU'LL RECEIVE A VALENTINE...
SOMEBODY HAS TO MAKE UP THOSE OLD LEGENDS, DON'T THEY?
SCHULZ

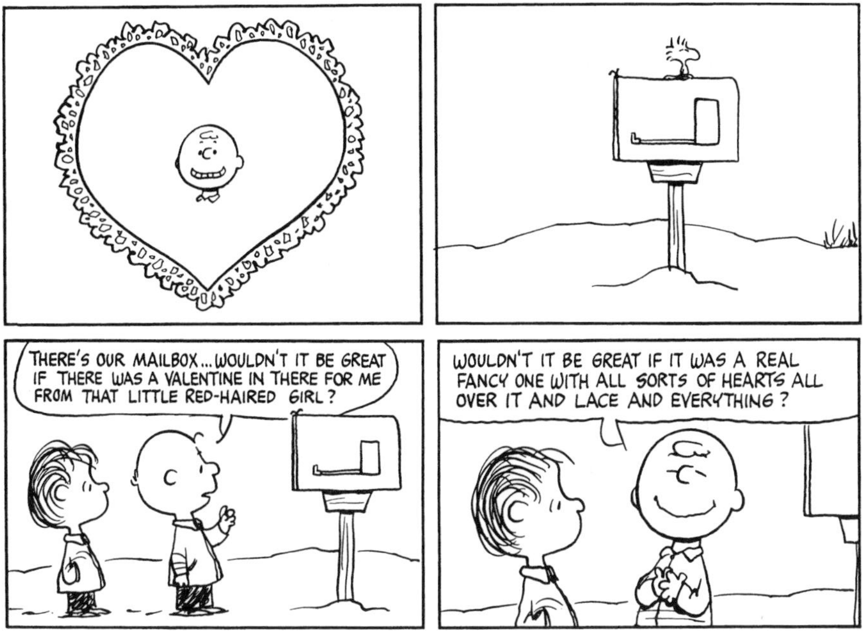
THERE'S OUR MAILBOX... WOULDN'T IT BE GREAT IF THERE WAS A VALENTINE IN THERE FOR ME FROM THAT LITTLE RED-HAIRED GIRL?
WOULDN'T IT BE GREAT IF IT WAS A REAL FANCY ONE WITH ALL SORTS OF HEARTS ALL OVER IT AND LACE AND EVERYTHING?

A Valentine for Charlie Brown

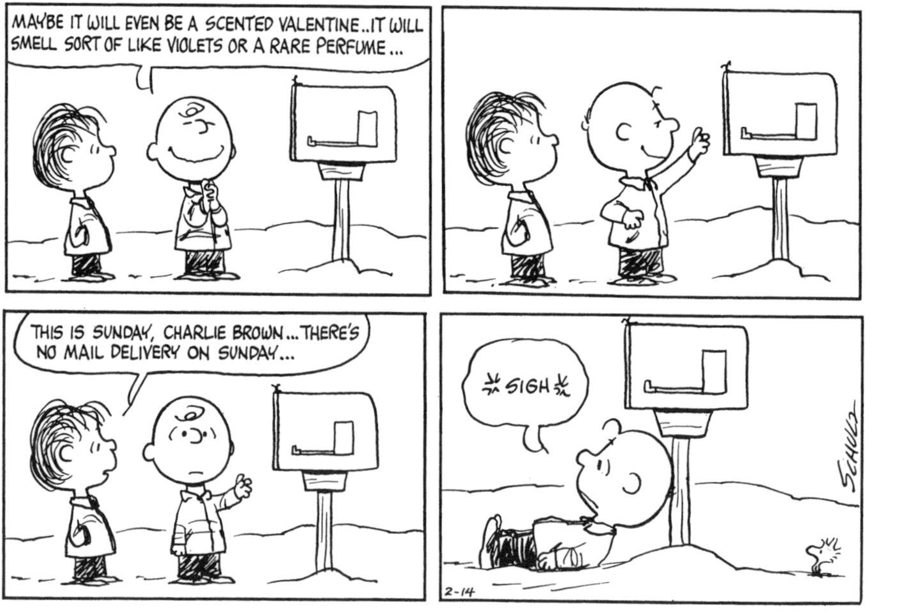
MAYBE IT WILL EVEN BE A SCENTED VALENTINE..IT WILL SMELL SORT OF LIKE VIOLETS OR A RARE PERFUME...
THIS IS SUNDAY, CHARLIE BROWN... THERE'S NO MAIL DELIVERY ON SUNDAY...
SIGH
SCHULZ
2-14

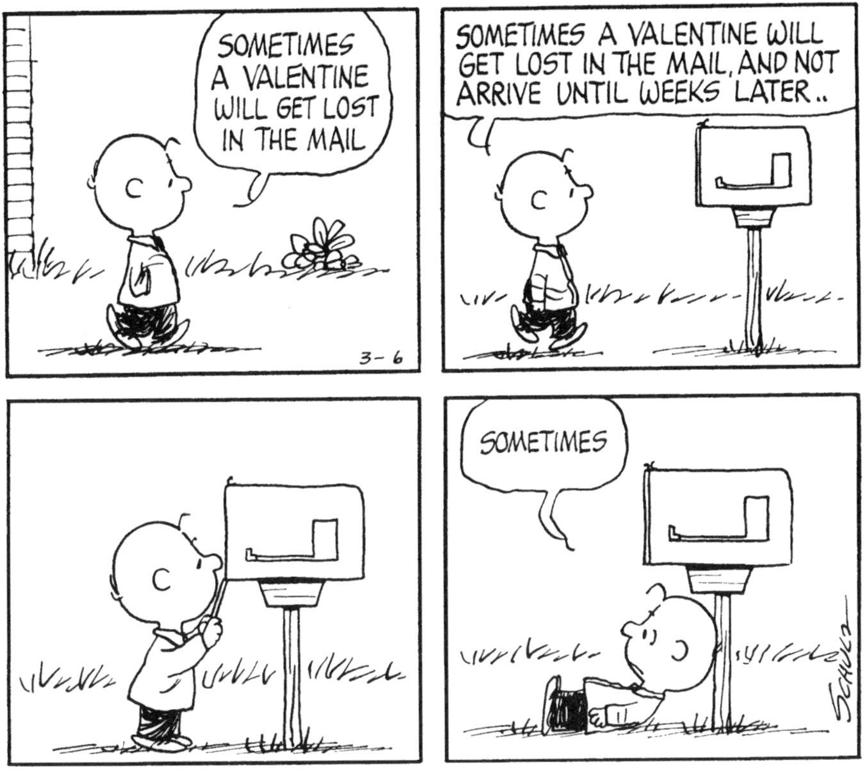
SOMETIMES A VALENTINE WILL GET LOST IN THE MAIL
3-6
SOMETIMES A VALENTINE WILL GET LOST IN THE MAIL, AND NOT ARRIVE UNTIL WEEKS LATER..
SOMETIMES
SCHULZ

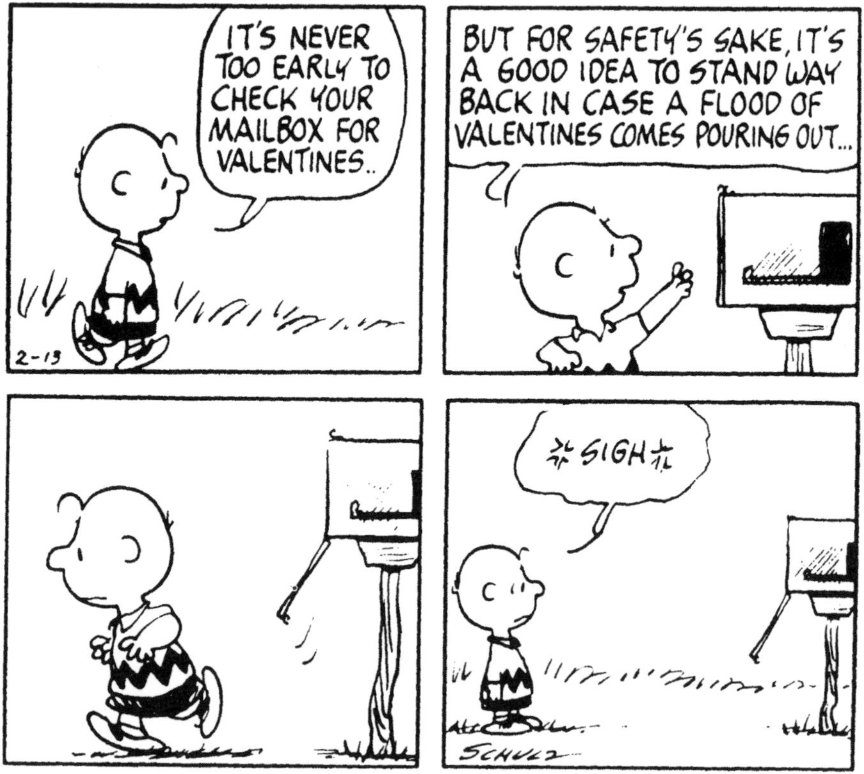
IT'S NEVER TOO EARLY TO CHECK YOUR MAILBOX FOR VALENTINES..
2-13
BUT FOR SAFETY'S SAKE, IT'S A GOOD IDEA TO STAND WAY BACK IN CASE A FLOOD OF VALENTINES COMES POURING OUT...
SIGH
SCHULZ

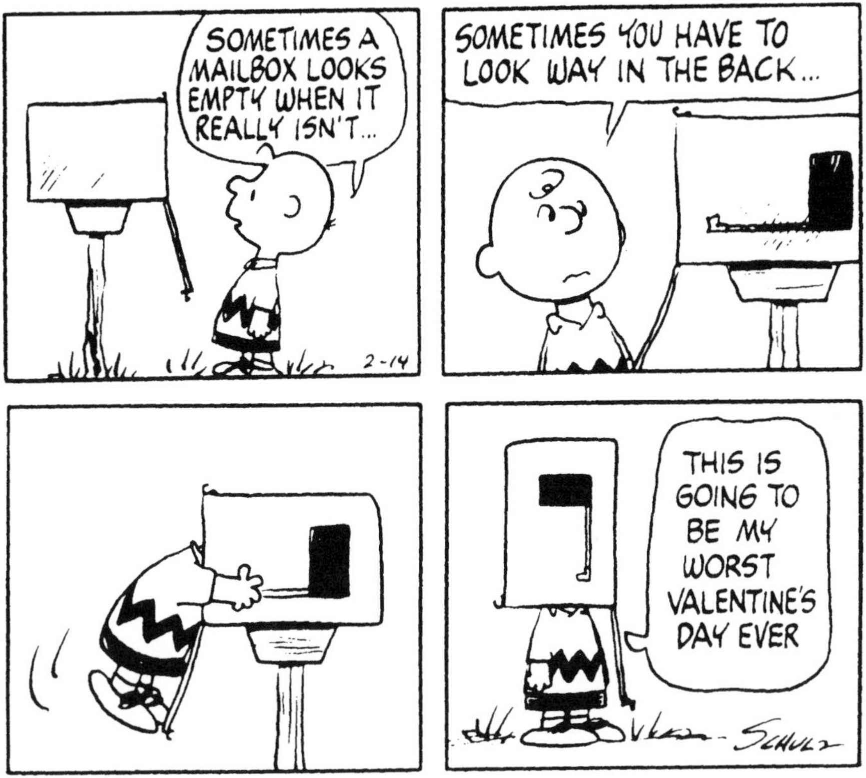
SOMETIMES A MAILBOX LOOKS EMPTY WHEN IT REALLY ISN'T...
2-14
SOMETIMES YOU HAVE TO LOOK WAY IN THE BACK...
THIS IS GOING TO BE MY WORST VALENTINE'S DAY EVER
SCHULZ

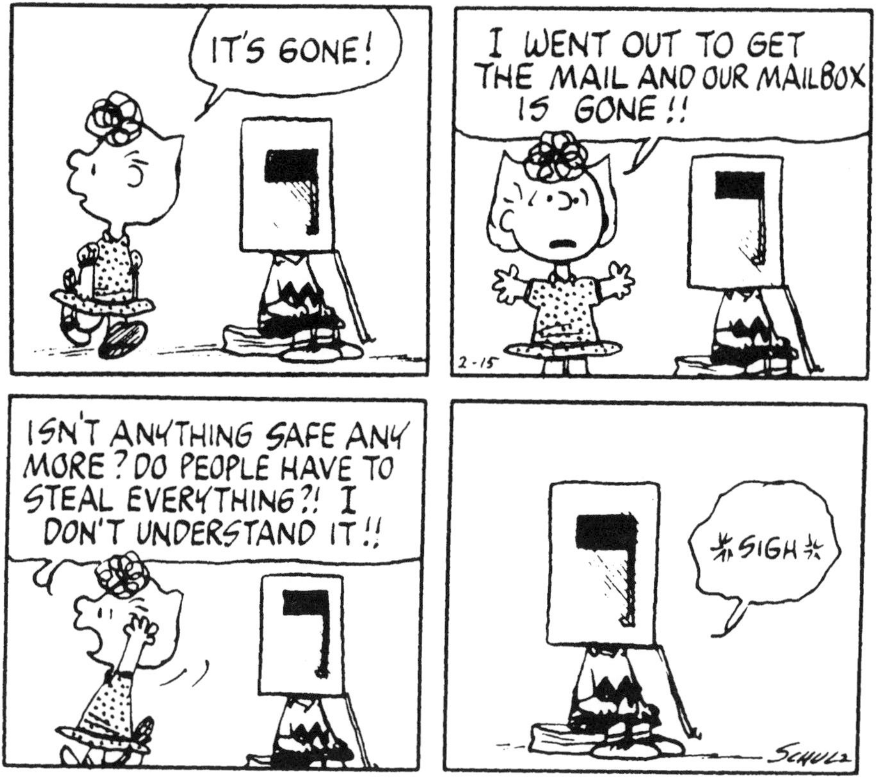
IT'S GONE!
I WENT OUT TO GET THE MAIL AND OUR MAILBOX IS GONE!!
2-15
ISN'T ANYTHING SAFE ANY MORE? DO PEOPLE HAVE TO STEAL EVERYTHING?! I DON'T UNDERSTAND IT!!
SIGH
SCHULZ

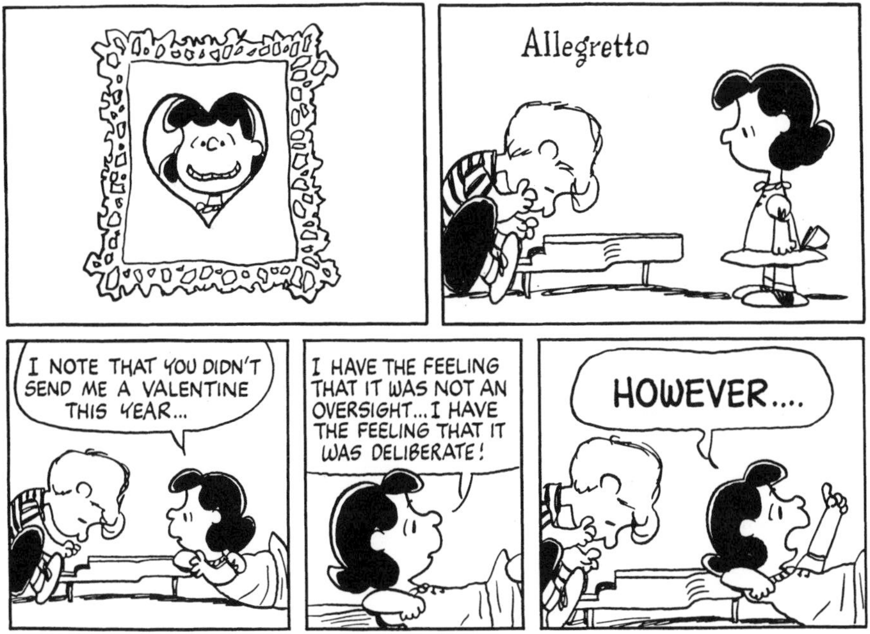
Allegretto
I NOTE THAT YOU DIDN'T SEND ME A VALENTINE THIS YEAR...
I HAVE THE FEELING THAT IT WAS NOT AN OVERSIGHT...I HAVE THE FEELING THAT IT WAS DELIBERATE!
HOWEVER....

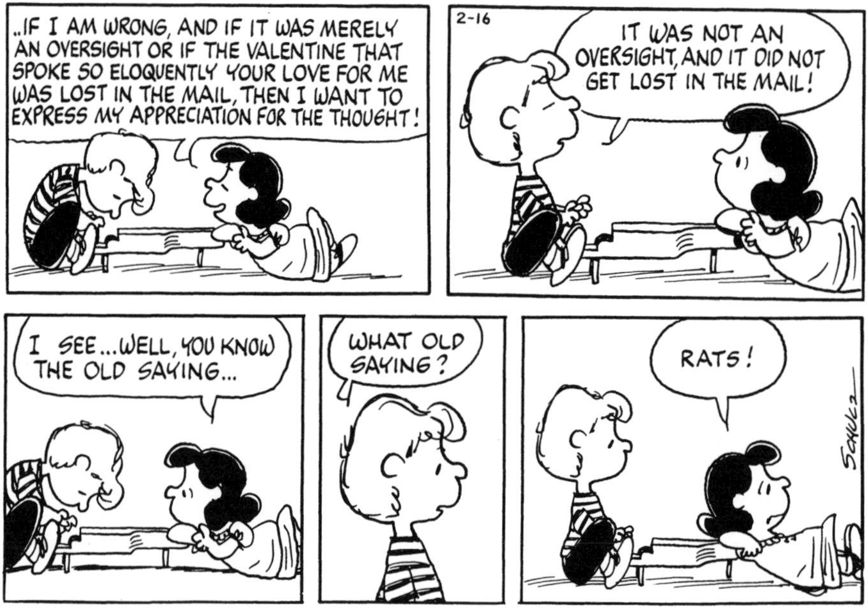
..IF I AM WRONG, AND IF IT WAS MERELY AN OVERSIGHT OR IF THE VALENTINE THAT SPOKE SO ELOQUENTLY YOUR LOVE FOR ME WAS LOST IN THE MAIL, THEN I WANT TO EXPRESS MY APPRECIATION FOR THE THOUGHT!
2-16
IT WAS NOT AN OVERSIGHT, AND IT DID NOT GET LOST IN THE MAIL!
I SEE...WELL, YOU KNOW THE OLD SAYING...
WHAT OLD SAYING?
RATS!
SCHULZ

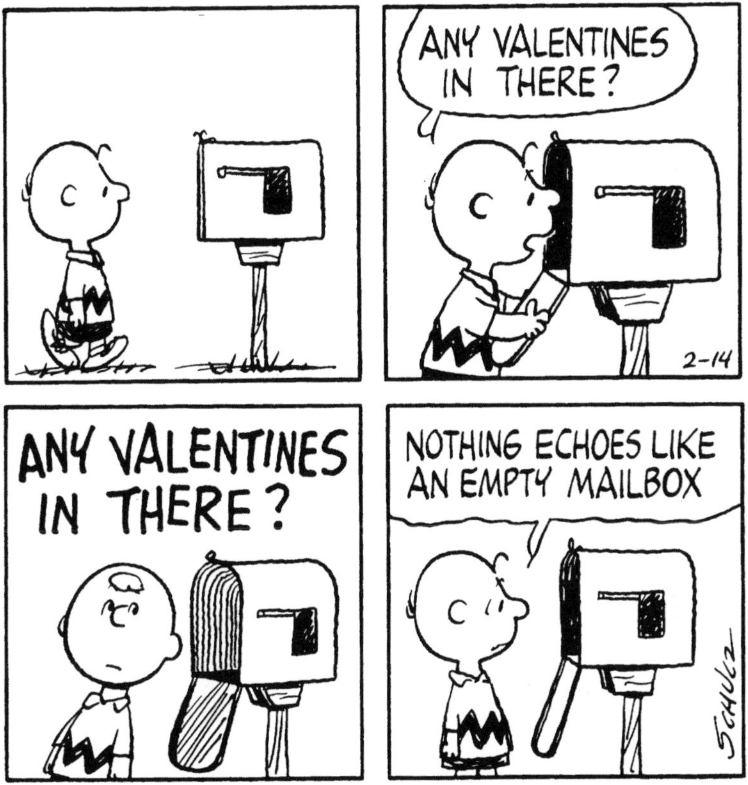
ANY VALENTINES IN THERE?
2-14
ANY VALENTINES IN THERE?
NOTHING ECHOES LIKE AN EMPTY MAILBOX
SCHULZ

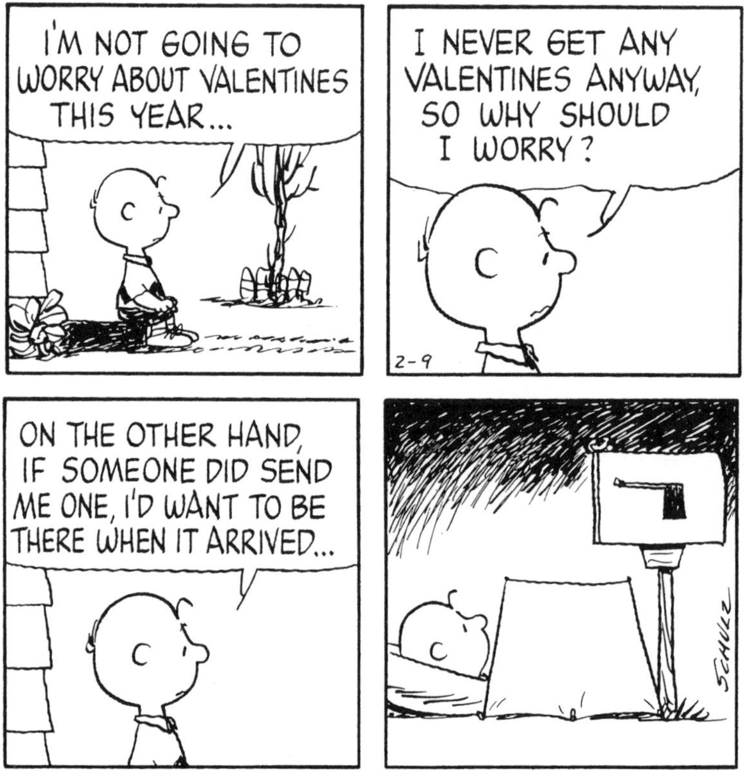
I'M NOT GOING TO WORRY ABOUT VALENTINES THIS YEAR...
I NEVER GET ANY VALENTINES ANYWAY, SO WHY SHOULD I WORRY?
2-9
ON THE OTHER HAND, IF SOMEONE DID SEND ME ONE, I'D WANT TO BE THERE WHEN IT ARRIVED...
SCHULZ

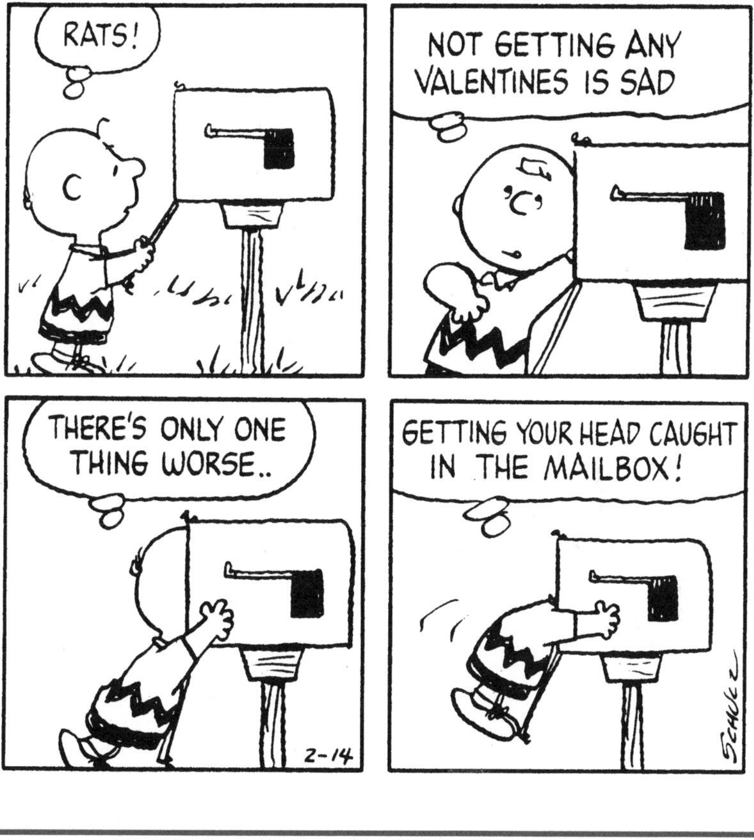
RATS!
NOT GETTING ANY VALENTINES IS SAD
THERE'S ONLY ONE THING WORSE..
GETTING YOUR HEAD CAUGHT IN THE MAILBOX!
2-14
SCHULZ

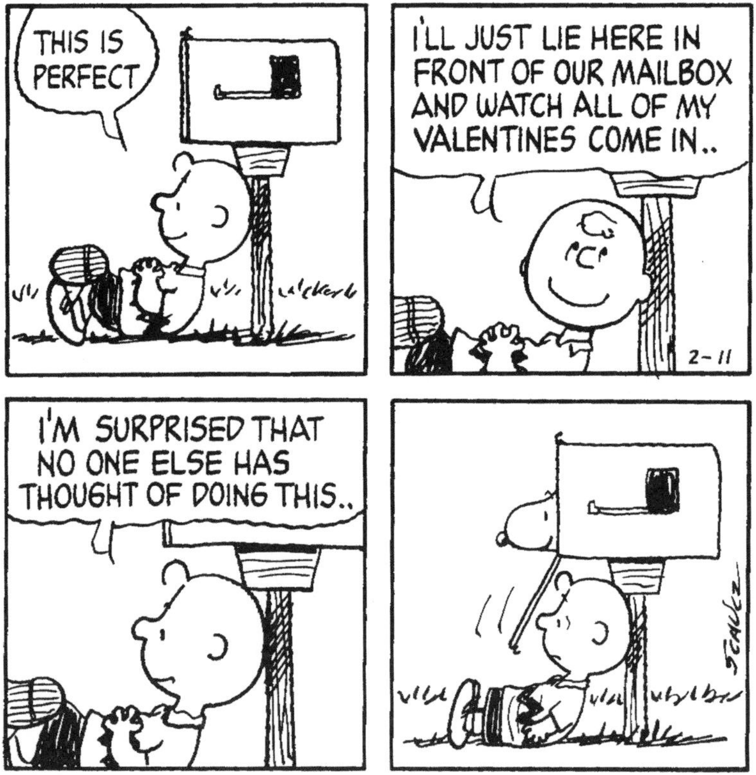
THIS IS PERFECT
I'LL JUST LIE HERE IN FRONT OF OUR MAILBOX AND WATCH ALL OF MY VALENTINES COME IN..
2-11
I'M SURPRISED THAT NO ONE ELSE HAS THOUGHT OF DOING THIS..
SCHULZ

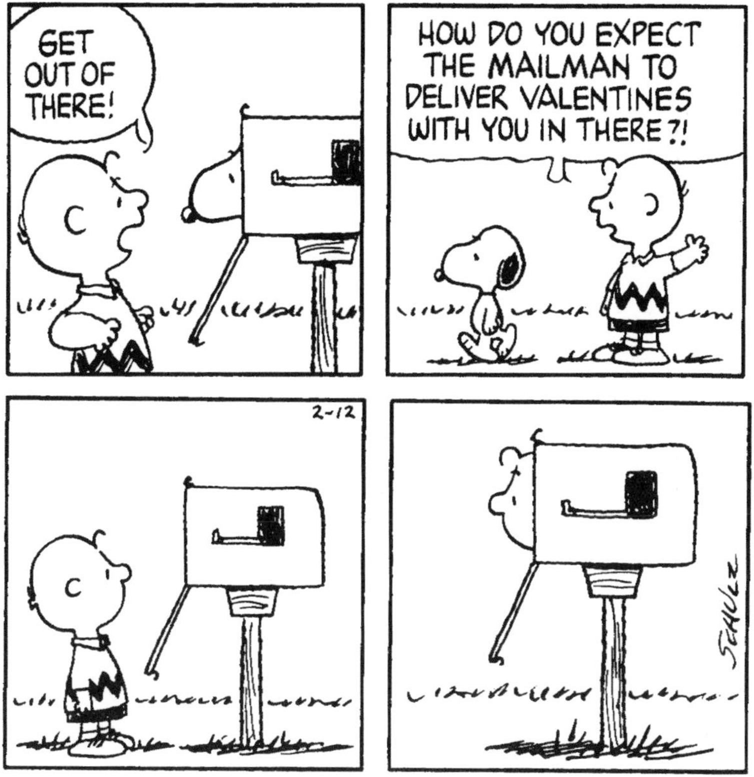
GET OUT OF THERE!
HOW DO YOU EXPECT THE MAILMAN TO DELIVER VALENTINES WITH YOU IN THERE?!
2-12
SCHULZ

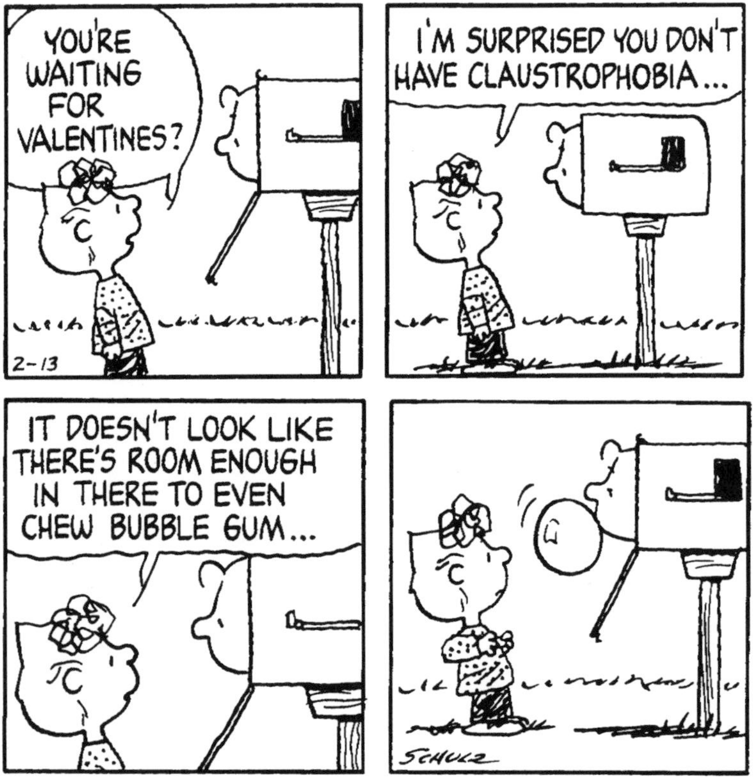
YOU'RE WAITING FOR VALENTINES?
2-13
I'M SURPRISED YOU DON'T HAVE CLAUSTROPHOBIA...
IT DOESN'T LOOK LIKE THERE'S ROOM ENOUGH IN THERE TO EVEN CHEW BUBBLE GUM...
SCHULZ

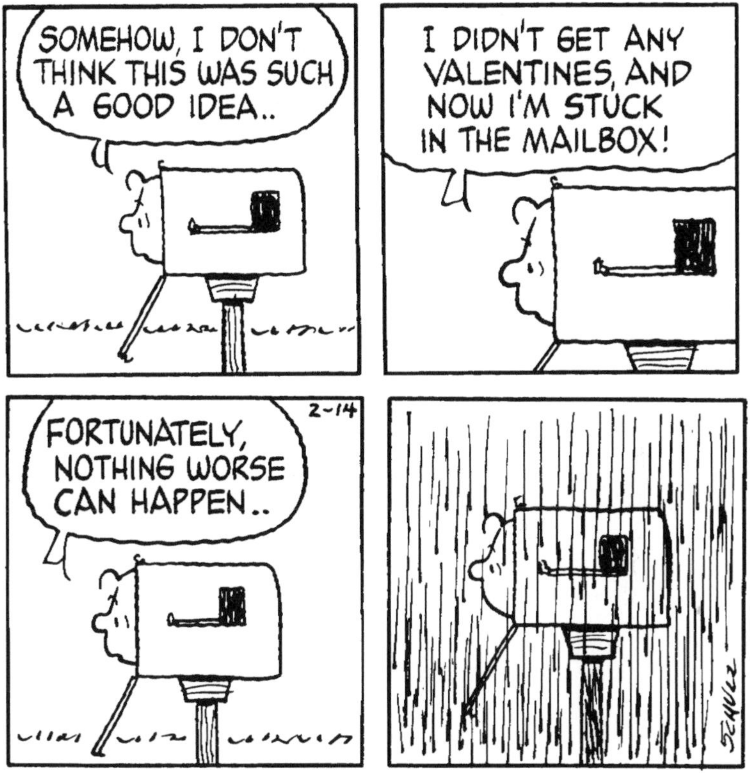
SOMEHOW, I DON'T THINK THIS WAS SUCH A GOOD IDEA..
I DIDN'T GET ANY VALENTINES, AND NOW I'M STUCK IN THE MAILBOX!
2-14
FORTUNATELY, NOTHING WORSE CAN HAPPEN..
SCHULZ

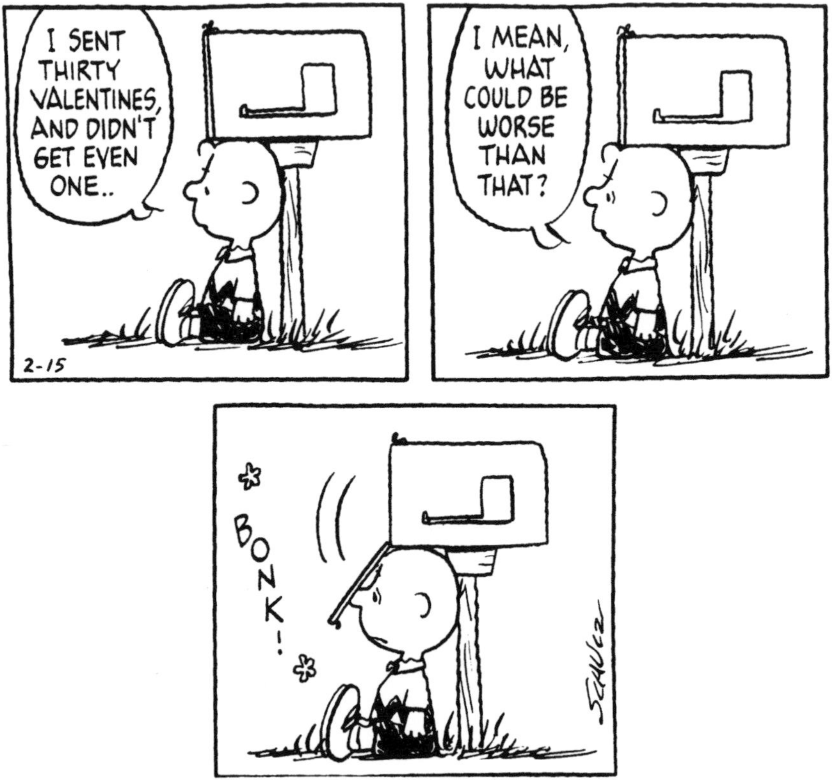
I SENT THIRTY VALENTINES, AND DIDN'T GET EVEN ONE..
2-15
I MEAN, WHAT COULD BE WORSE THAN THAT?
BONK!
SCHULZ

The Little Red-Haired Girl

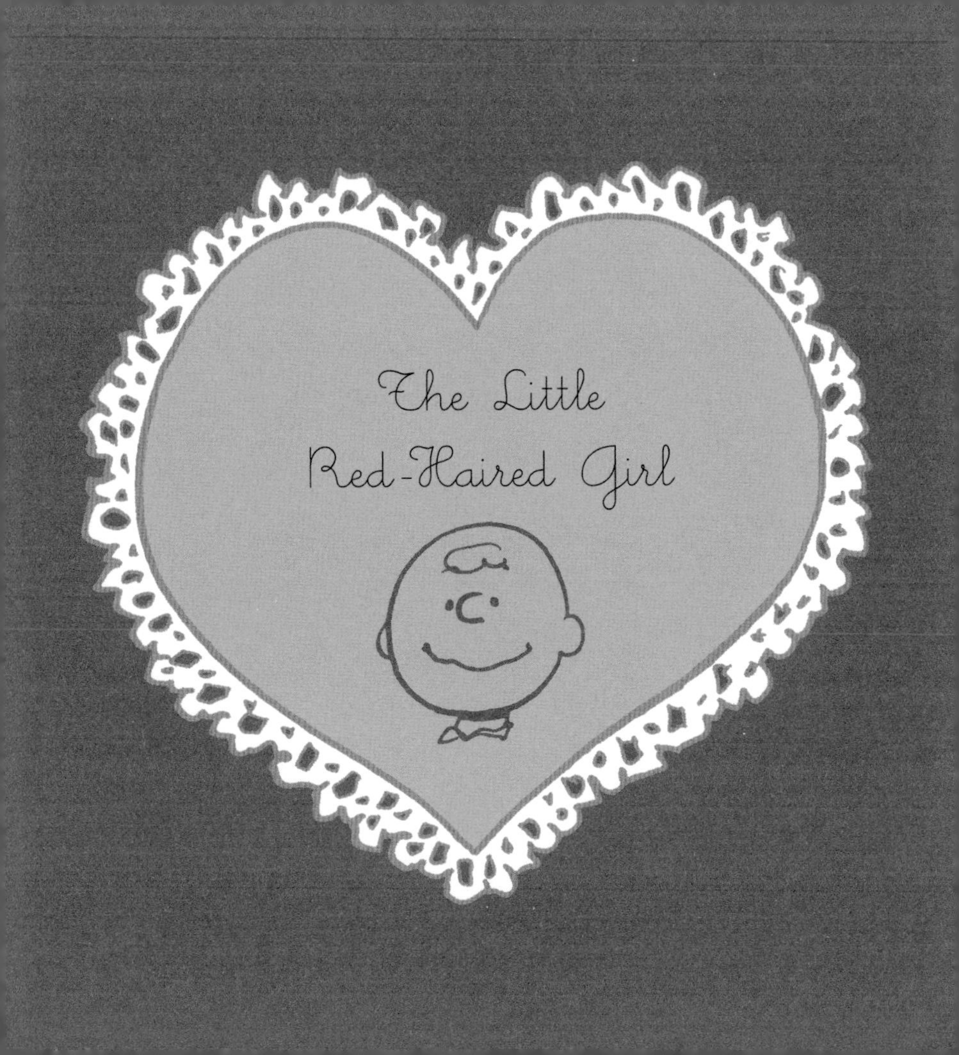

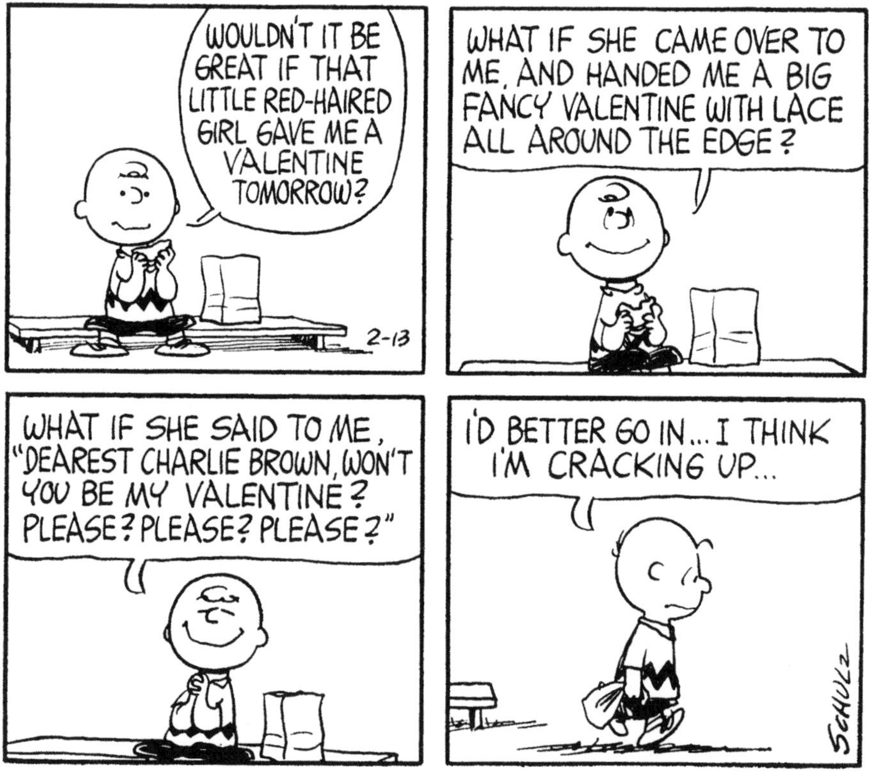
WOULDN'T IT BE GREAT IF THAT LITTLE RED-HAIRED GIRL GAVE ME A VALENTINE TOMORROW?
2-13
WHAT IF SHE CAME OVER TO ME, AND HANDED ME A BIG FANCY VALENTINE WITH LACE ALL AROUND THE EDGE?
WHAT IF SHE SAID TO ME, "DEAREST CHARLIE BROWN, WON'T YOU BE MY VALENTINE? PLEASE? PLEASE? PLEASE?"
I'D BETTER GO IN... I THINK I'M CRACKING UP...
SCHULZ

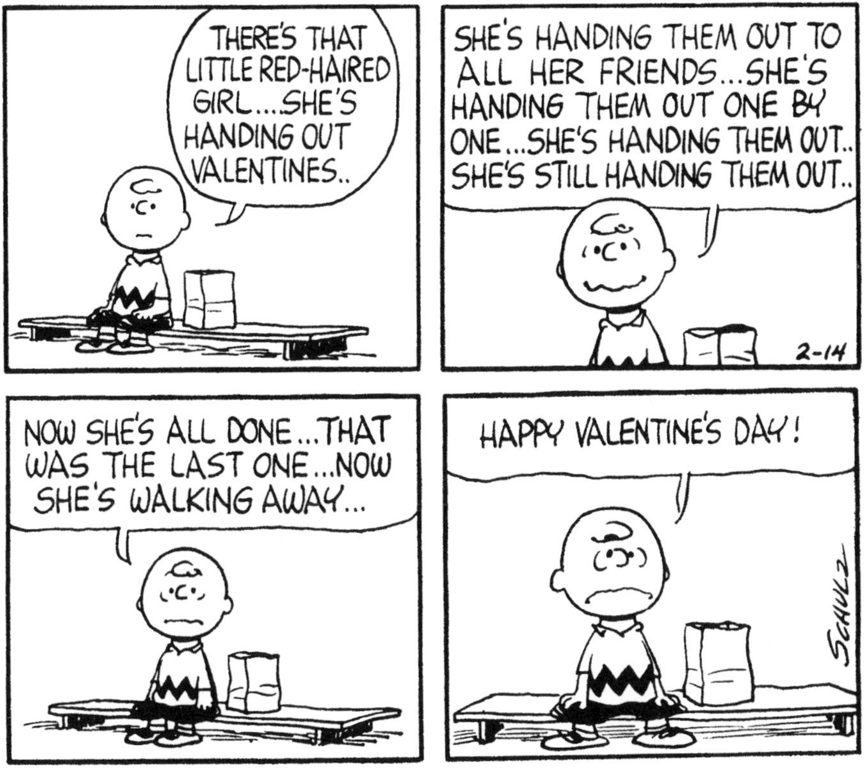
THERE'S THAT LITTLE RED-HAIRED GIRL....SHE'S HANDING OUT VALENTINES..
SHE'S HANDING THEM OUT TO ALL HER FRIENDS...SHE'S HANDING THEM OUT ONE BY ONE...SHE'S HANDING THEM OUT.. SHE'S STILL HANDING THEM OUT..
2-14
NOW SHE'S ALL DONE...THAT WAS THE LAST ONE...NOW SHE'S WALKING AWAY...
HAPPY VALENTINE'S DAY!
SCHULZ

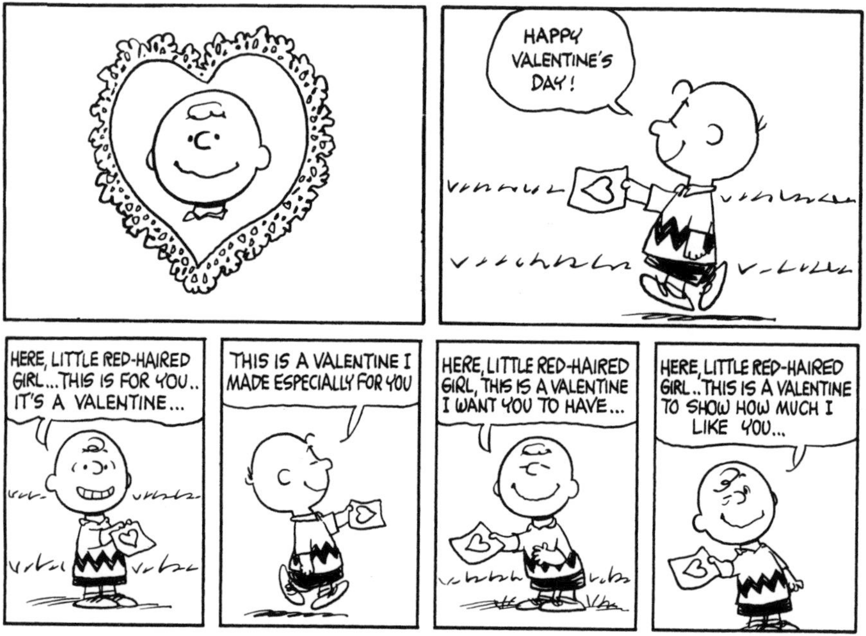
HAPPY VALENTINE'S DAY!
HERE, LITTLE RED-HAIRED GIRL... THIS IS FOR YOU.. IT'S A VALENTINE...
THIS IS A VALENTINE I MADE ESPECIALLY FOR YOU
HERE, LITTLE RED-HAIRED GIRL, THIS IS A VALENTINE I WANT YOU TO HAVE...
HERE, LITTLE RED-HAIRED GIRL.. THIS IS A VALENTINE TO SHOW HOW MUCH I LIKE YOU...

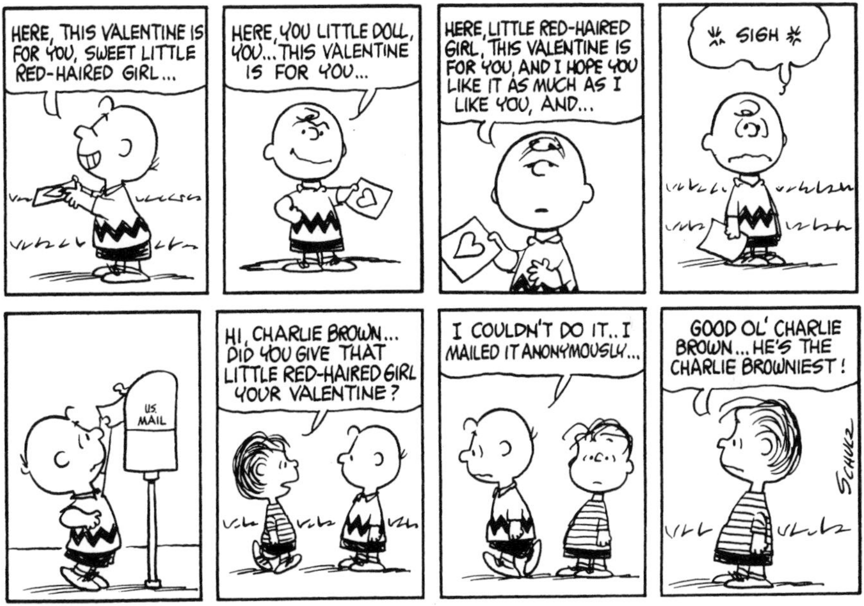
HERE, THIS VALENTINE IS FOR YOU, SWEET LITTLE RED-HAIRED GIRL...
HERE, YOU LITTLE DOLL, YOU... THIS VALENTINE IS FOR YOU...
HERE, LITTLE RED-HAIRED GIRL, THIS VALENTINE IS FOR YOU, AND I HOPE YOU LIKE IT AS MUCH AS I LIKE YOU, AND...
SIGH
U.S. MAIL
HI, CHARLIE BROWN... DID YOU GIVE THAT LITTLE RED-HAIRED GIRL YOUR VALENTINE?
I COULDN'T DO IT.. I MAILED IT ANONYMOUSLY...
GOOD OL' CHARLIE BROWN... HE'S THE CHARLIE BROWNIEST!
SCHULZ

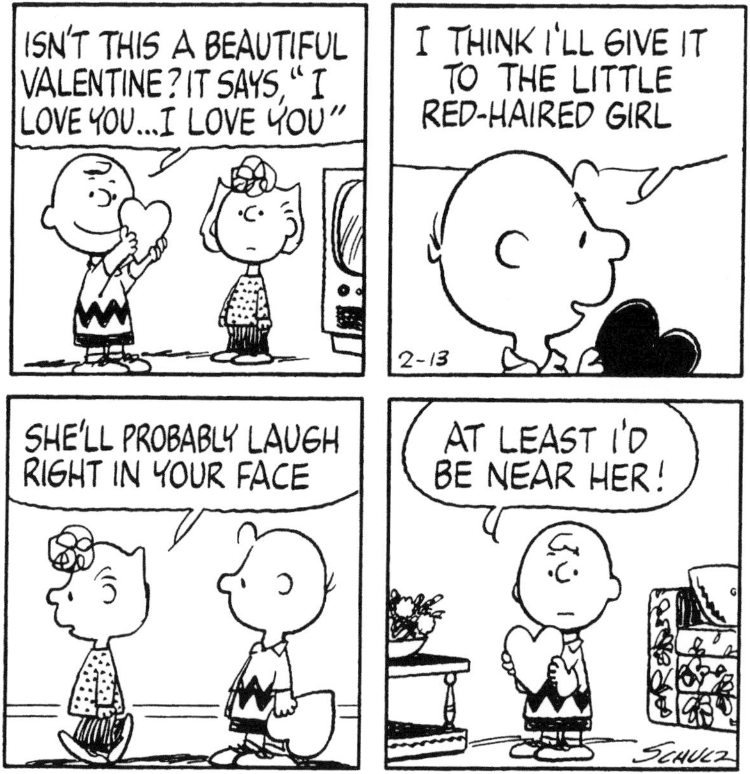
ISN'T THIS A BEAUTIFUL VALENTINE? IT SAYS, "I LOVE YOU...I LOVE YOU"
I THINK I'LL GIVE IT TO THE LITTLE RED-HAIRED GIRL
2-13
SHE'LL PROBABLY LAUGH RIGHT IN YOUR FACE
AT LEAST I'D BE NEAR HER!
SCHULZ

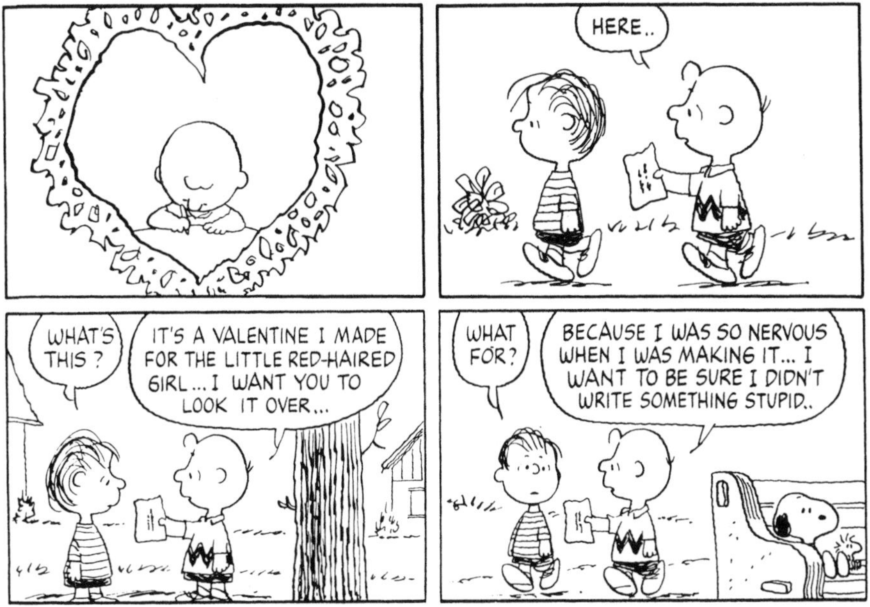
HERE..
WHAT'S THIS ?
IT'S A VALENTINE I MADE FOR THE LITTLE RED-HAIRED GIRL... I WANT YOU TO LOOK IT OVER...
WHAT FOR?
BECAUSE I WAS SO NERVOUS WHEN I WAS MAKING IT... I WANT TO BE SURE I DIDN'T WRITE SOMETHING STUPID..

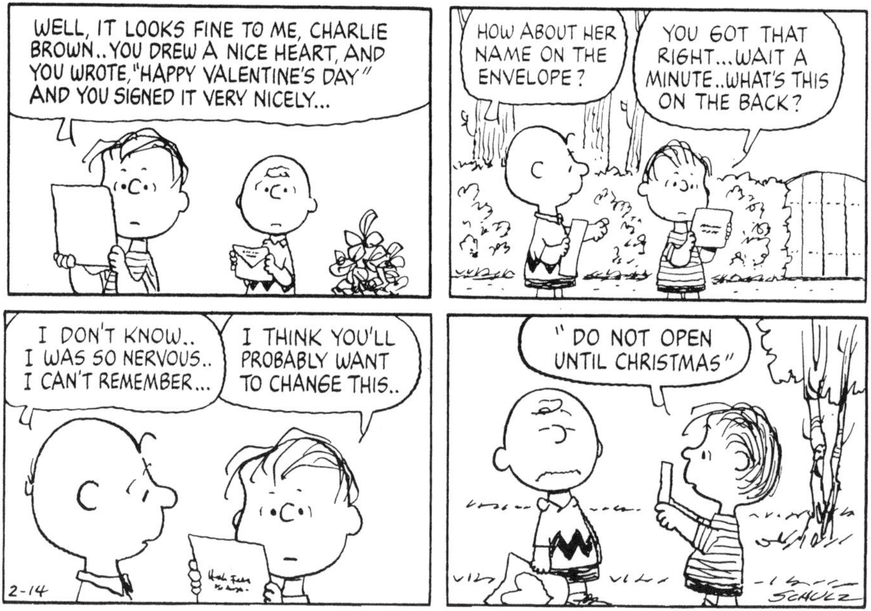
WELL, IT LOOKS FINE TO ME, CHARLIE BROWN.. YOU DREW A NICE HEART, AND YOU WROTE, "HAPPY VALENTINE'S DAY" AND YOU SIGNED IT VERY NICELY...
HOW ABOUT HER NAME ON THE ENVELOPE?
YOU GOT THAT RIGHT...WAIT A MINUTE..WHAT'S THIS ON THE BACK?
I DON'T KNOW.. I WAS SO NERVOUS.. I CAN'T REMEMBER...
I THINK YOU'LL PROBABLY WANT TO CHANGE THIS..
"DO NOT OPEN UNTIL CHRISTMAS"
2-14
SCHULZ

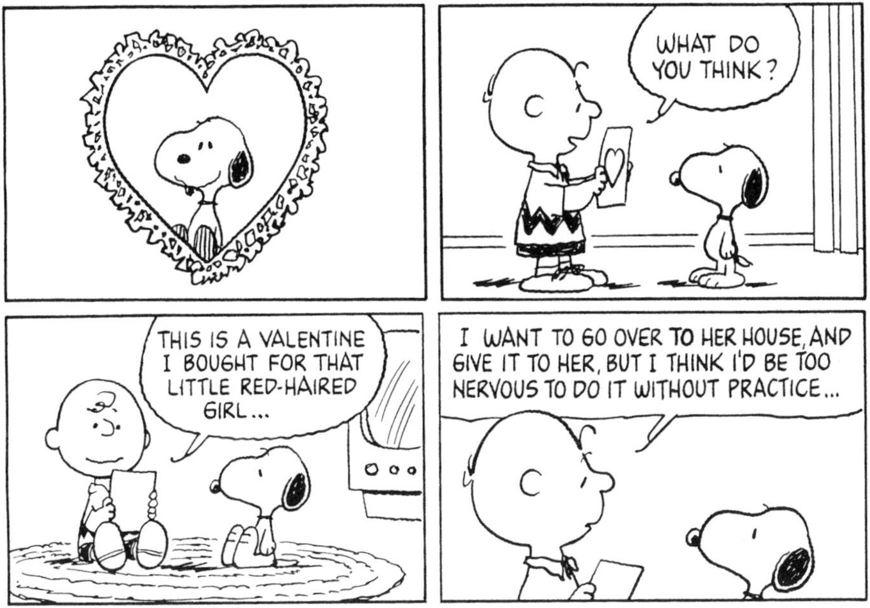
WHAT DO YOU THINK?
THIS IS A VALENTINE I BOUGHT FOR THAT LITTLE RED-HAIRED GIRL...
I WANT TO GO OVER TO HER HOUSE, AND GIVE IT TO HER, BUT I THINK I'D BE TOO NERVOUS TO DO IT WITHOUT PRACTICE...

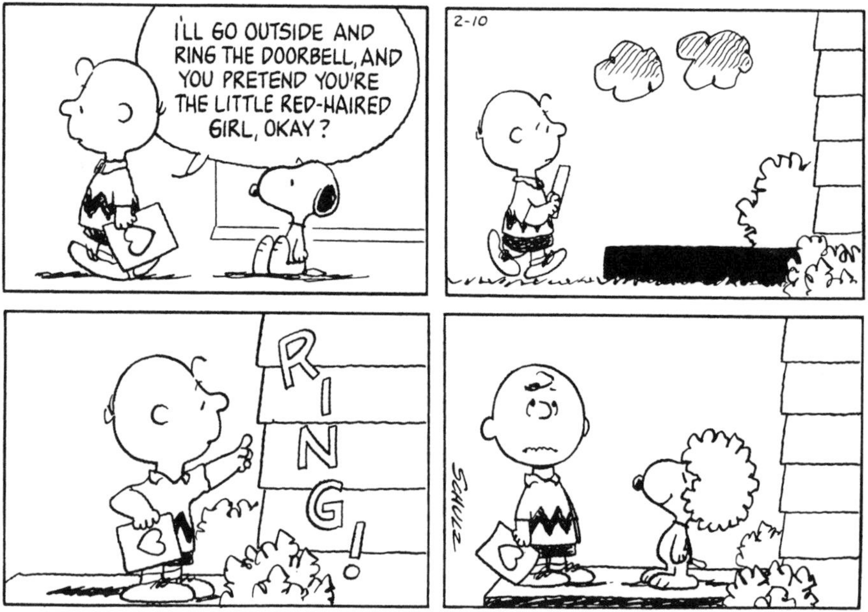
I'LL GO OUTSIDE AND RING THE DOORBELL, AND YOU PRETEND YOU'RE THE LITTLE RED-HAIRED GIRL, OKAY?
2-10
RING!
SCHULZ

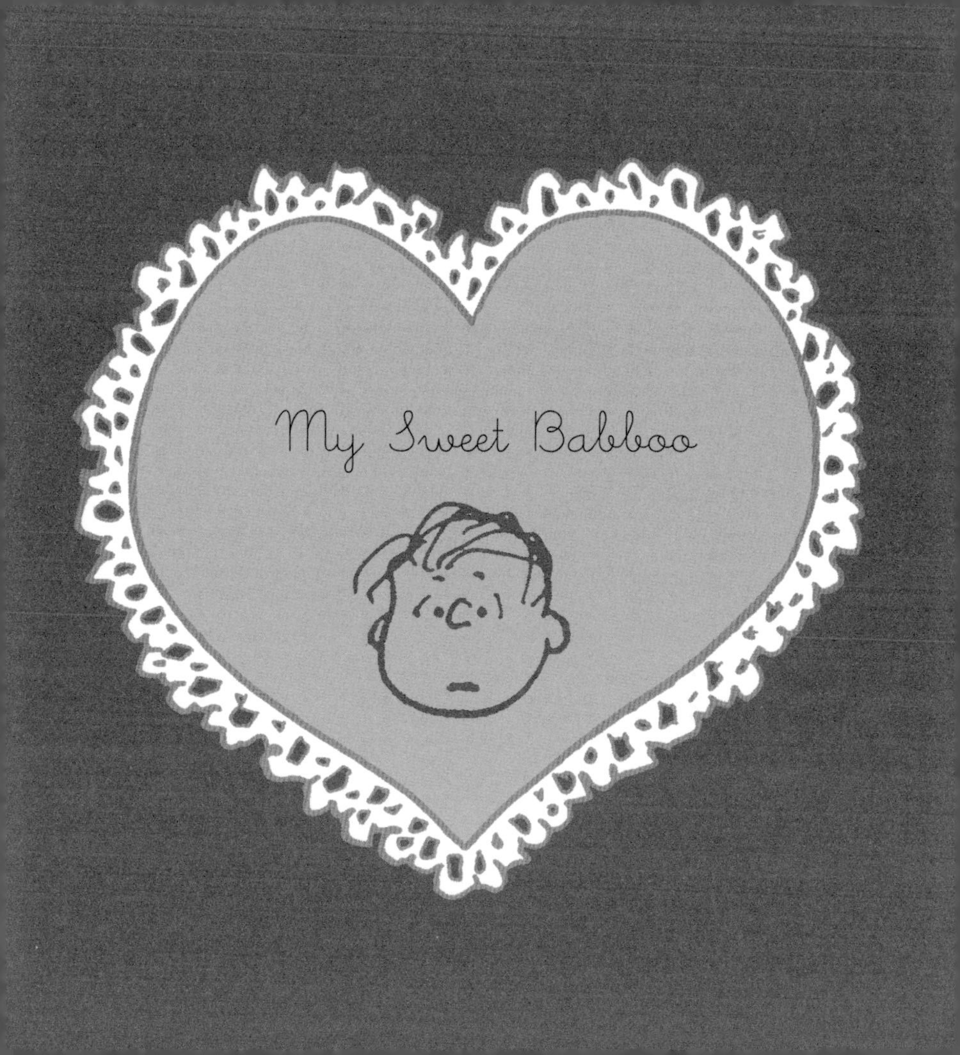
My Sweet Babboo

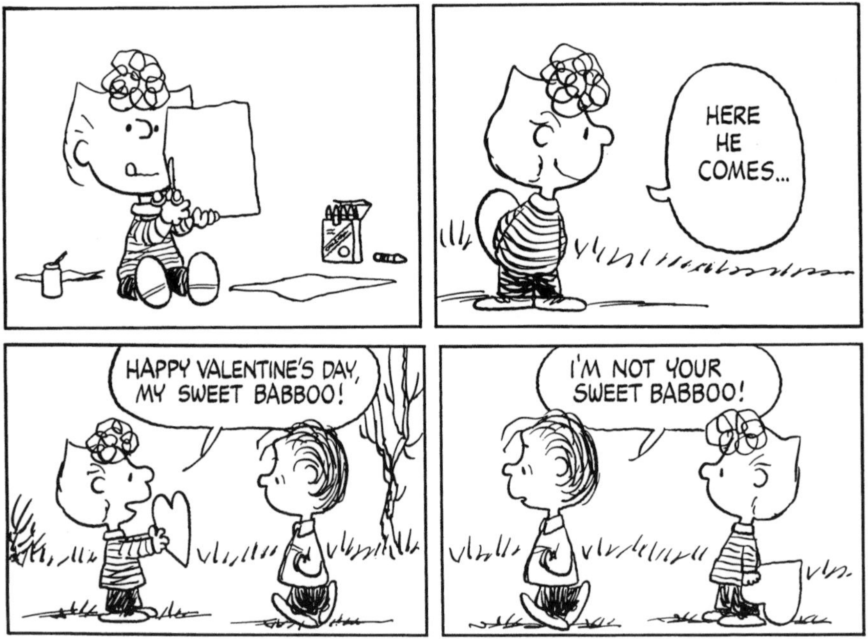
HERE HE COMES...
HAPPY VALENTINE'S DAY, MY SWEET BABBOO!
I'M NOT YOUR SWEET BABBOO!

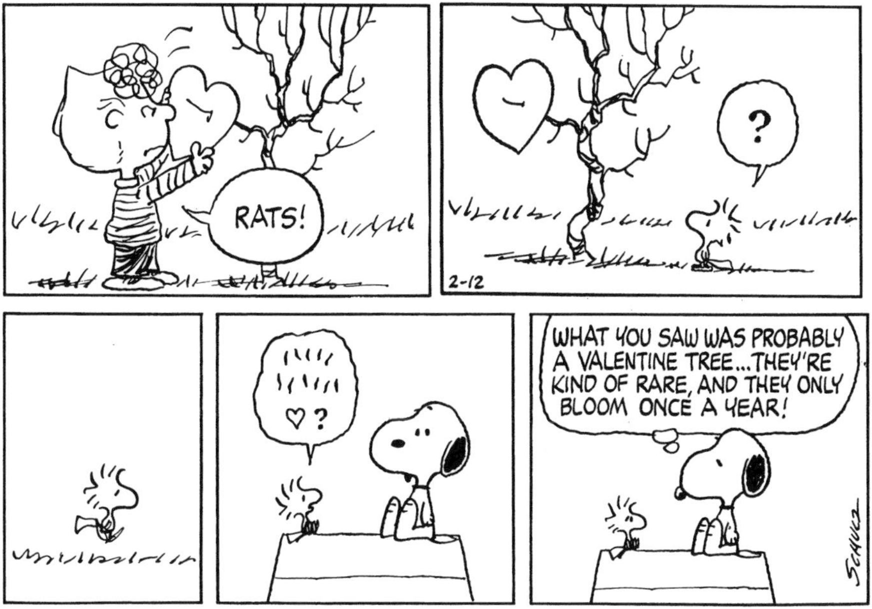
RATS!
?
2-12
♡ ?
WHAT YOU SAW WAS PROBABLY A VALENTINE TREE...THEY'RE KIND OF RARE, AND THEY ONLY BLOOM ONCE A YEAR!
SCHULZ

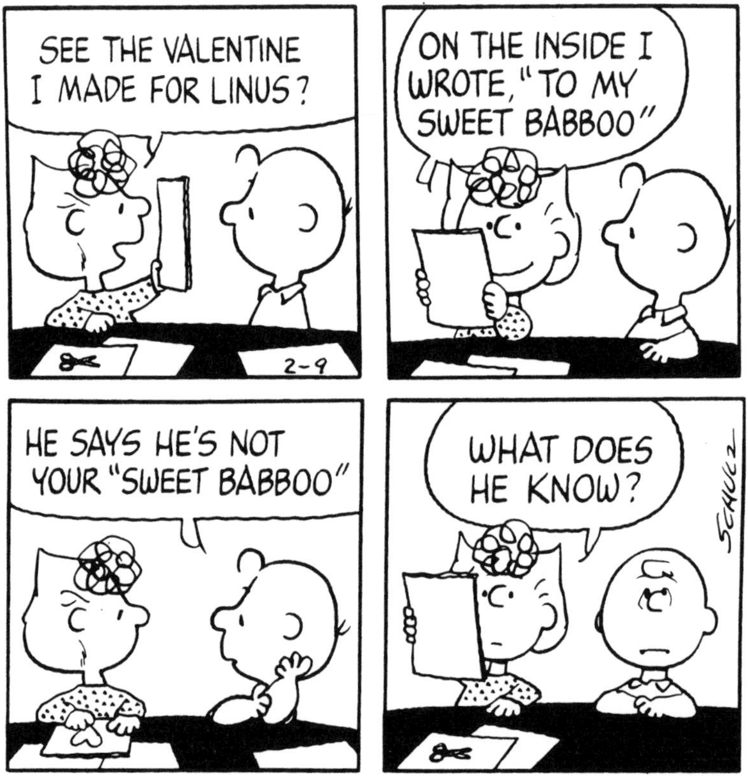
SEE THE VALENTINE I MADE FOR LINUS?
2-9
ON THE INSIDE I WROTE, "TO MY SWEET BABBOO"
HE SAYS HE'S NOT YOUR "SWEET BABBOO"
WHAT DOES HE KNOW?
SCHULZ

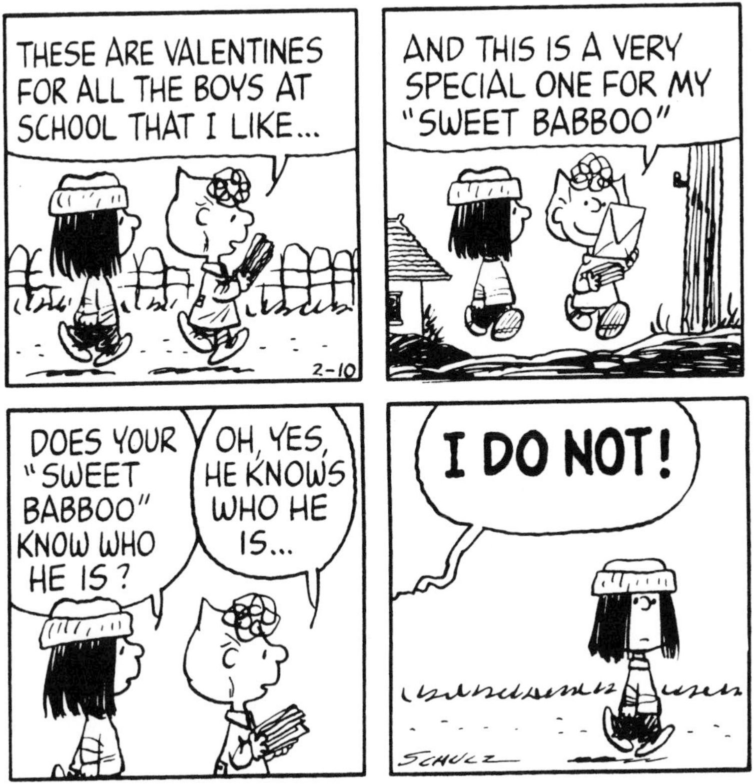
THESE ARE VALENTINES FOR ALL THE BOYS AT SCHOOL THAT I LIKE...
2-10
AND THIS IS A VERY SPECIAL ONE FOR MY "SWEET BABBOO"
DOES YOUR "SWEET BABBOO" KNOW WHO HE IS?
OH, YES, HE KNOWS WHO HE IS...
I DO NOT!
SCHULZ

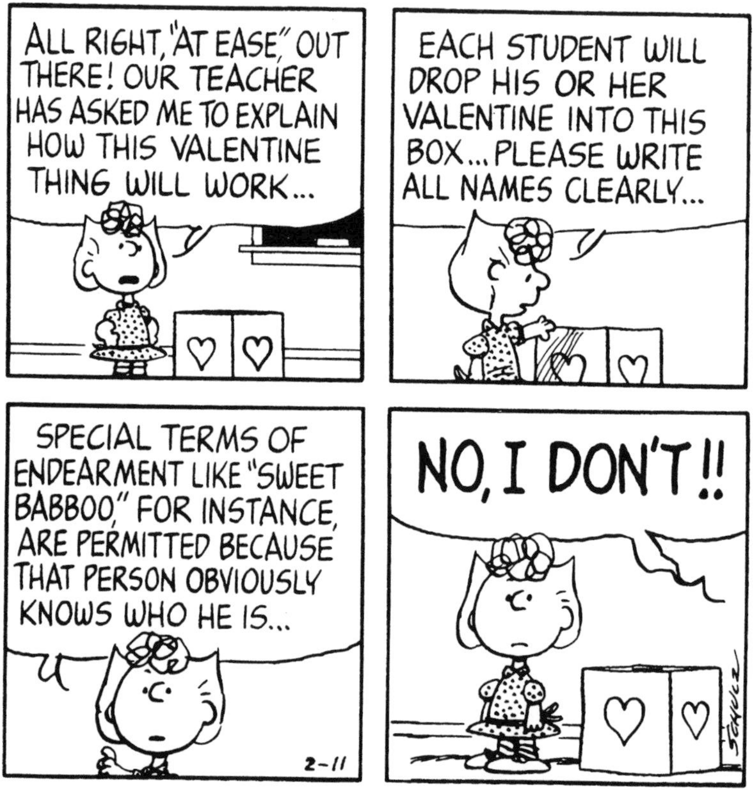
ALL RIGHT, "AT EASE" OUT THERE! OUR TEACHER HAS ASKED ME TO EXPLAIN HOW THIS VALENTINE THING WILL WORK...
EACH STUDENT WILL DROP HIS OR HER VALENTINE INTO THIS BOX... PLEASE WRITE ALL NAMES CLEARLY...
SPECIAL TERMS OF ENDEARMENT LIKE "SWEET BABBOO," FOR INSTANCE, ARE PERMITTED BECAUSE THAT PERSON OBVIOUSLY KNOWS WHO HE IS...
2-11
NO, I DON'T!!
SCHULZ

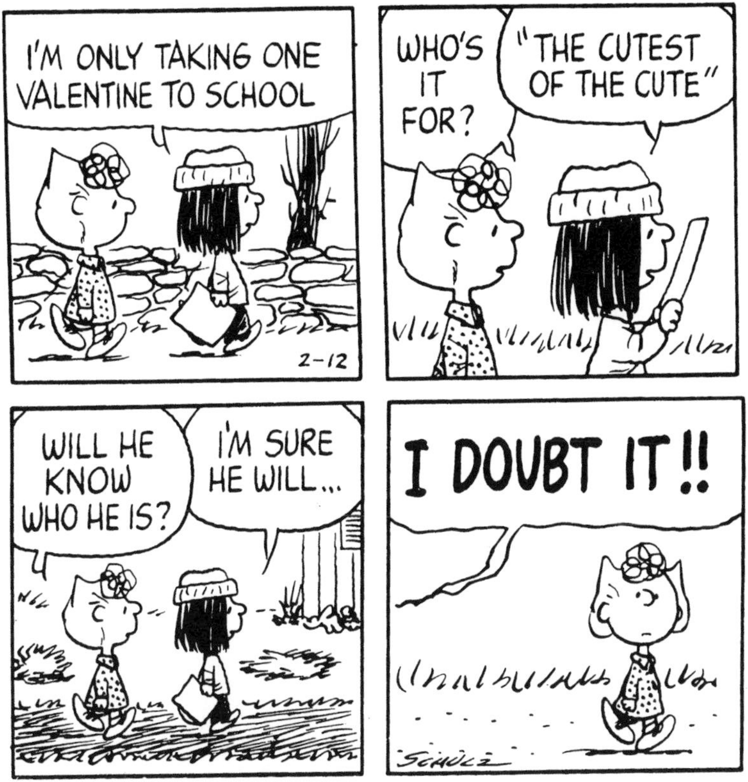
I'M ONLY TAKING ONE VALENTINE TO SCHOOL
2-12
WHO'S IT FOR?
"THE CUTEST OF THE CUTE"
WILL HE KNOW WHO HE IS?
I'M SURE HE WILL...
I DOUBT IT!!
SCHULZ

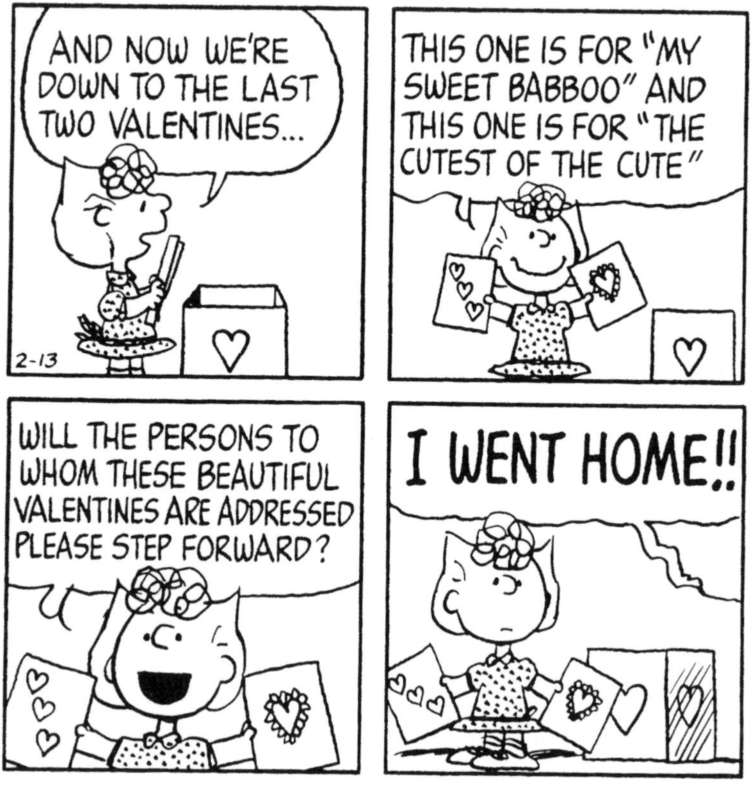
AND NOW WE'RE DOWN TO THE LAST TWO VALENTINES...
2-13
THIS ONE IS FOR "MY SWEET BABBOO" AND THIS ONE IS FOR "THE CUTEST OF THE CUTE"
WILL THE PERSONS TO WHOM THESE BEAUTIFUL VALENTINES ARE ADDRESSED PLEASE STEP FORWARD?
I WENT HOME!!

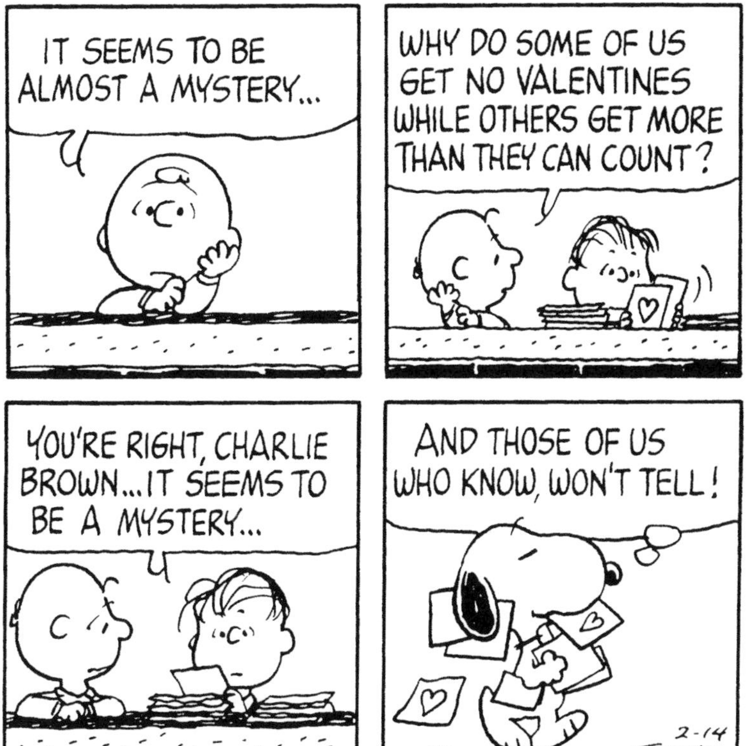
IT SEEMS TO BE ALMOST A MYSTERY...
WHY DO SOME OF US GET NO VALENTINES WHILE OTHERS GET MORE THAN THEY CAN COUNT?
YOU'RE RIGHT, CHARLIE BROWN...IT SEEMS TO BE A MYSTERY...
AND THOSE OF US WHO KNOW, WON'T TELL!
2-14
SCHULZ

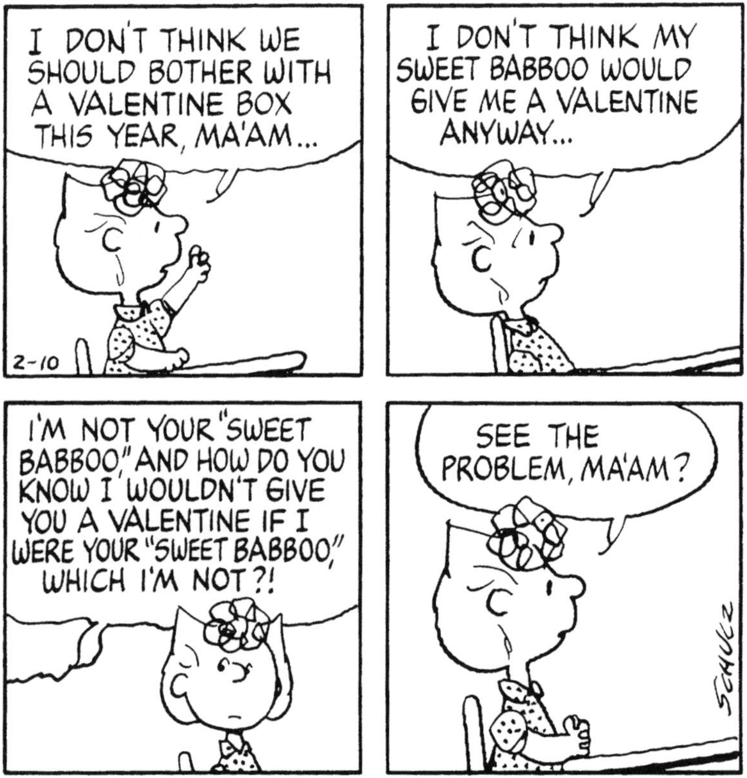
I DON'T THINK WE SHOULD BOTHER WITH A VALENTINE BOX THIS YEAR, MA'AM...
2-10
I DON'T THINK MY SWEET BABBOO WOULD GIVE ME A VALENTINE ANYWAY...
I'M NOT YOUR "SWEET BABBOO" AND HOW DO YOU KNOW I WOULDN'T GIVE YOU A VALENTINE IF I WERE YOUR "SWEET BABBOO," WHICH I'M NOT?!
SEE THE PROBLEM, MA'AM?
SCHULZ

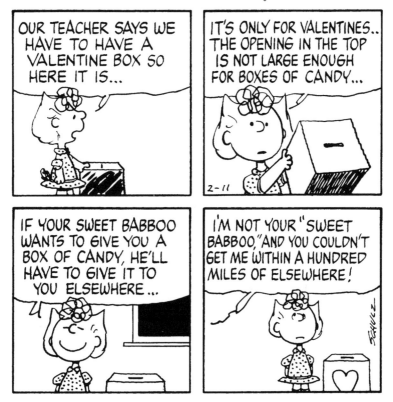

OUR TEACHER SAYS WE HAVE TO HAVE A VALENTINE BOX SO HERE IT IS...

IT'S ONLY FOR VALENTINES.. THE OPENING IN THE TOP IS NOT LARGE ENOUGH FOR BOXES OF CANDY...

2-11

IF YOUR SWEET BABBOO WANTS TO GIVE YOU A BOX OF CANDY, HE'LL HAVE TO GIVE IT TO YOU ELSEWHERE ...

I'M NOT YOUR "SWEET BABBOO," AND YOU COULDN'T GET ME WITHIN A HUNDRED MILES OF ELSEWHERE!

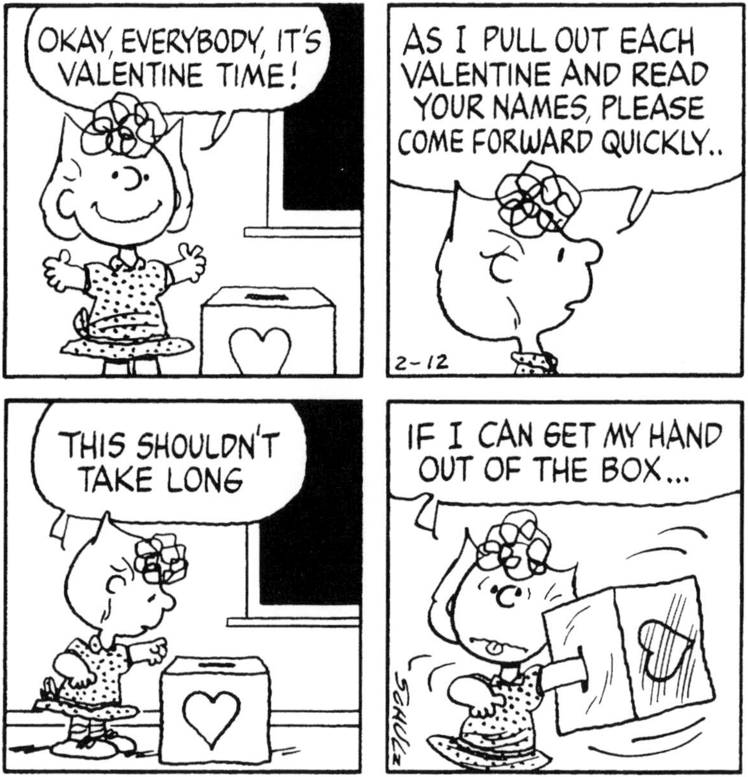
OKAY, EVERYBODY, IT'S VALENTINE TIME!
AS I PULL OUT EACH VALENTINE AND READ YOUR NAMES, PLEASE COME FORWARD QUICKLY..
2-12
THIS SHOULDN'T TAKE LONG
IF I CAN GET MY HAND OUT OF THE BOX...
SCHULZ

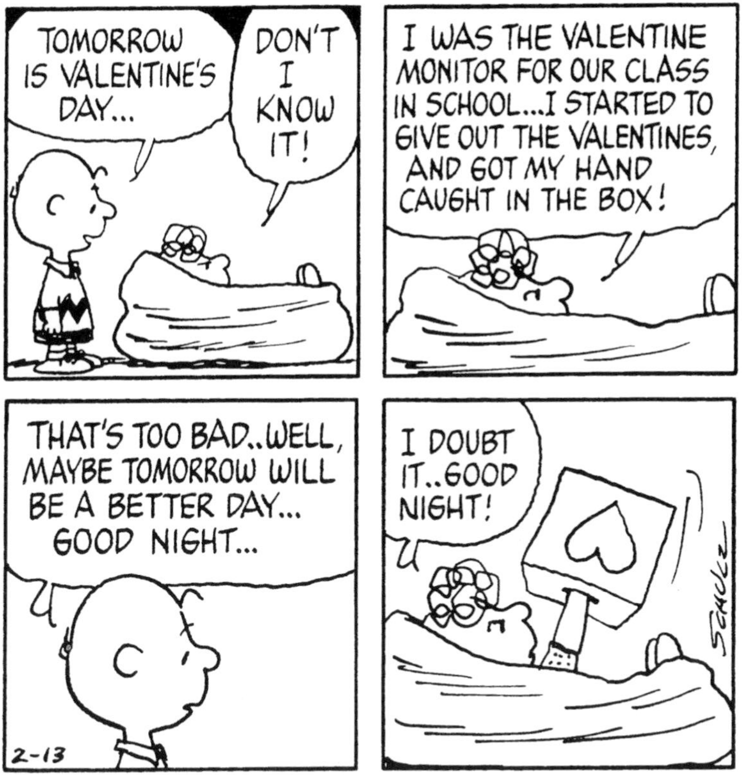
TOMORROW IS VALENTINE'S DAY...
DON'T I KNOW IT!
I WAS THE VALENTINE MONITOR FOR OUR CLASS IN SCHOOL...I STARTED TO GIVE OUT THE VALENTINES, AND GOT MY HAND CAUGHT IN THE BOX!
THAT'S TOO BAD..WELL, MAYBE TOMORROW WILL BE A BETTER DAY... GOOD NIGHT...
I DOUBT IT..GOOD NIGHT!
2-13
SCHULZ

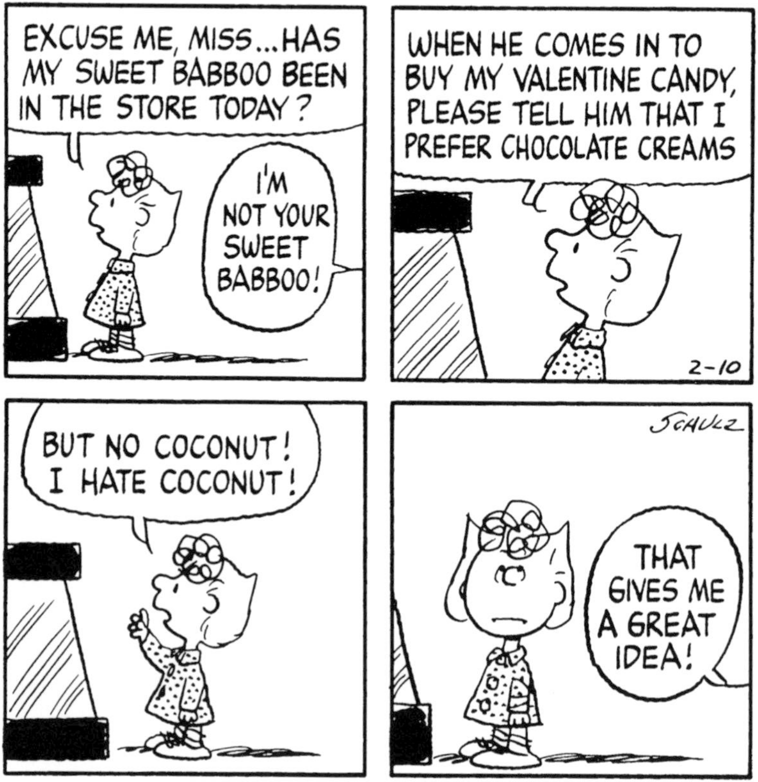
EXCUSE ME, MISS...HAS MY SWEET BABBOO BEEN IN THE STORE TODAY?
I'M NOT YOUR SWEET BABBOO!
WHEN HE COMES IN TO BUY MY VALENTINE CANDY, PLEASE TELL HIM THAT I PREFER CHOCOLATE CREAMS
2-10
BUT NO COCONUT! I HATE COCONUT!
SCHULZ
THAT GIVES ME A GREAT IDEA!

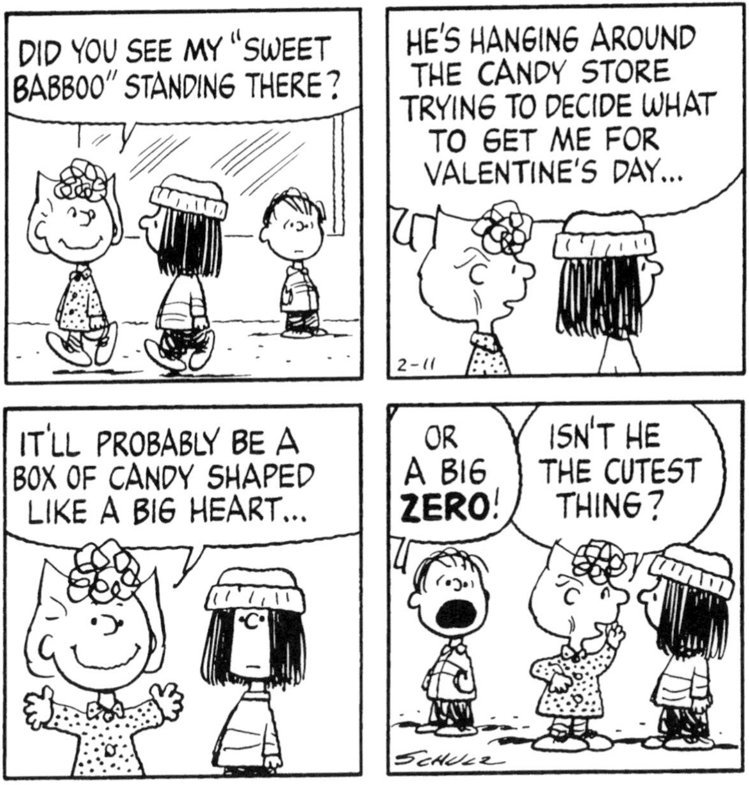
DID YOU SEE MY "SWEET BABBOO" STANDING THERE?
HE'S HANGING AROUND THE CANDY STORE TRYING TO DECIDE WHAT TO GET ME FOR VALENTINE'S DAY...
2-11
IT'LL PROBABLY BE A BOX OF CANDY SHAPED LIKE A BIG HEART...
ISN'T HE THE CUTEST THING?
OR A BIG **ZERO**!
SCHULZ

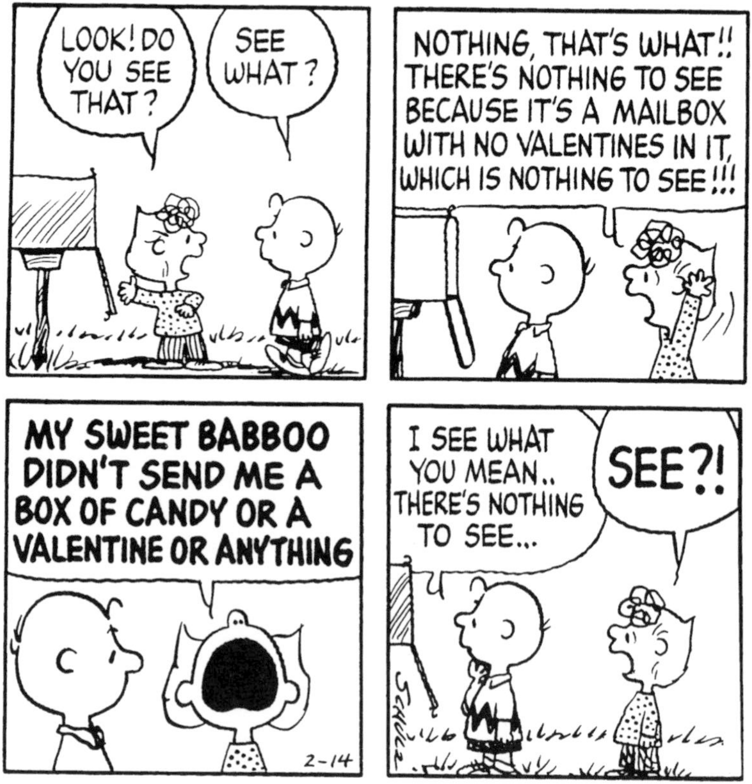
LOOK! DO YOU SEE THAT?
SEE WHAT?
NOTHING, THAT'S WHAT!! THERE'S NOTHING TO SEE BECAUSE IT'S A MAILBOX WITH NO VALENTINES IN IT, WHICH IS NOTHING TO SEE!!!
MY SWEET BABBOO DIDN'T SEND ME A BOX OF CANDY OR A VALENTINE OR ANYTHING
2-14
I SEE WHAT YOU MEAN.. THERE'S NOTHING TO SEE...
SEE?!
SCHULZ

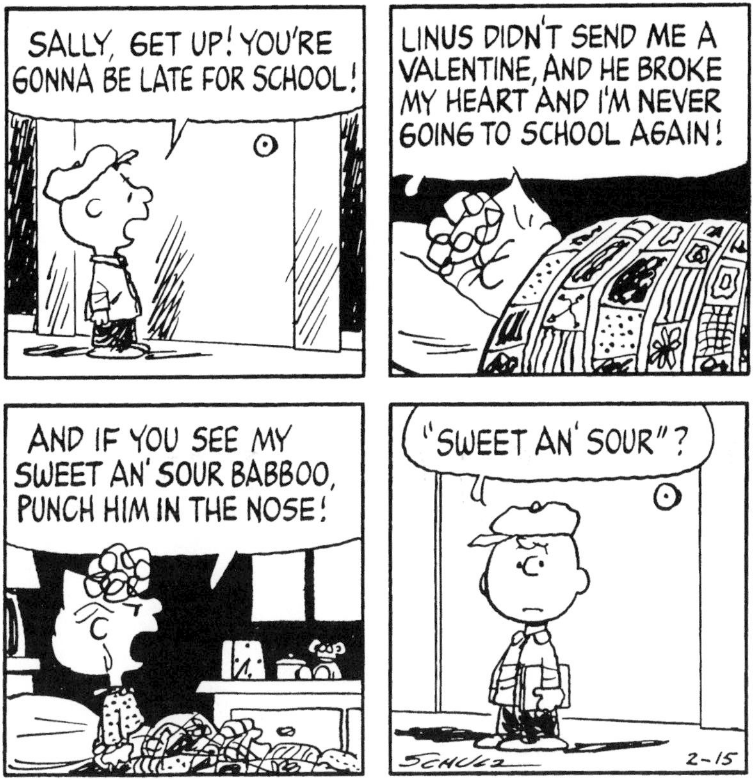
SALLY, GET UP! YOU'RE GONNA BE LATE FOR SCHOOL!
LINUS DIDN'T SEND ME A VALENTINE, AND HE BROKE MY HEART AND I'M NEVER GOING TO SCHOOL AGAIN!
AND IF YOU SEE MY SWEET AN' SOUR BABBOO, PUNCH HIM IN THE NOSE!
"SWEET AN' SOUR"?
SCHULZ
2-15

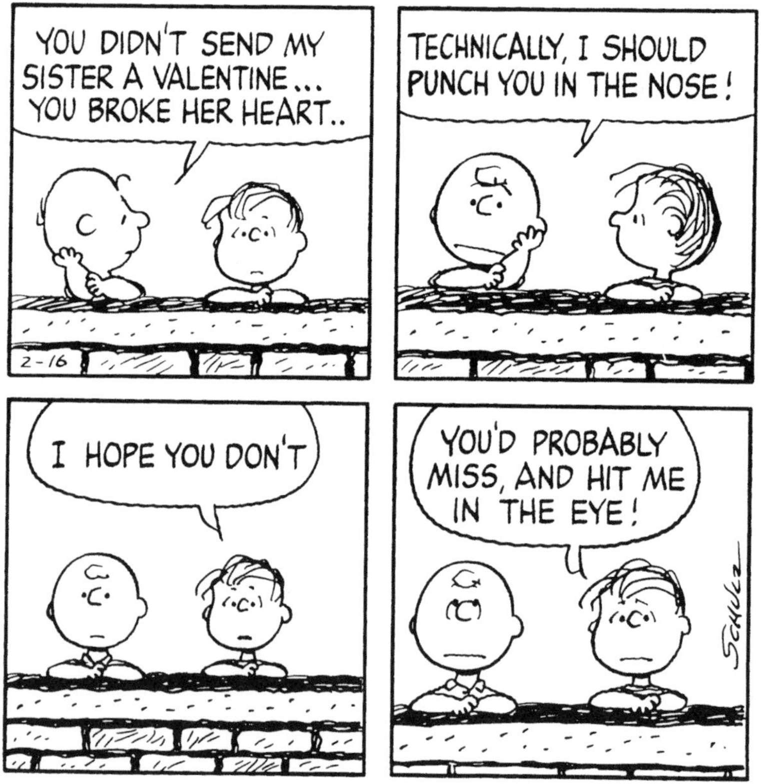
YOU DIDN'T SEND MY SISTER A VALENTINE... YOU BROKE HER HEART..
2-16
TECHNICALLY, I SHOULD PUNCH YOU IN THE NOSE!
I HOPE YOU DON'T
YOU'D PROBABLY MISS, AND HIT ME IN THE EYE!
SCHULZ

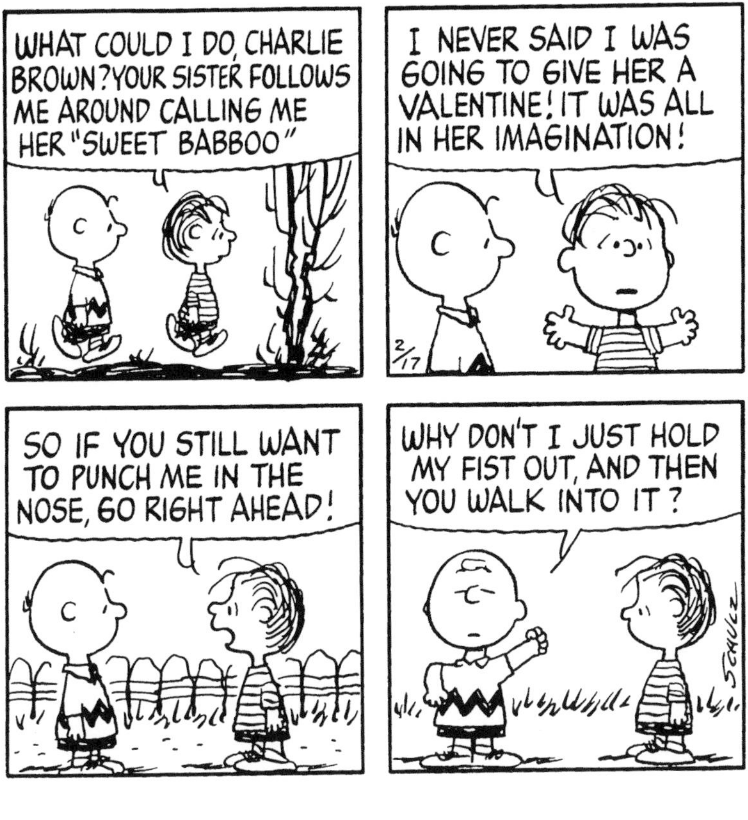
WHAT COULD I DO, CHARLIE BROWN? YOUR SISTER FOLLOWS ME AROUND CALLING ME HER "SWEET BABBOO"
I NEVER SAID I WAS GOING TO GIVE HER A VALENTINE! IT WAS ALL IN HER IMAGINATION!
2/17
SO IF YOU STILL WANT TO PUNCH ME IN THE NOSE, GO RIGHT AHEAD!
WHY DON'T I JUST HOLD MY FIST OUT, AND THEN YOU WALK INTO IT?
SCHULZ

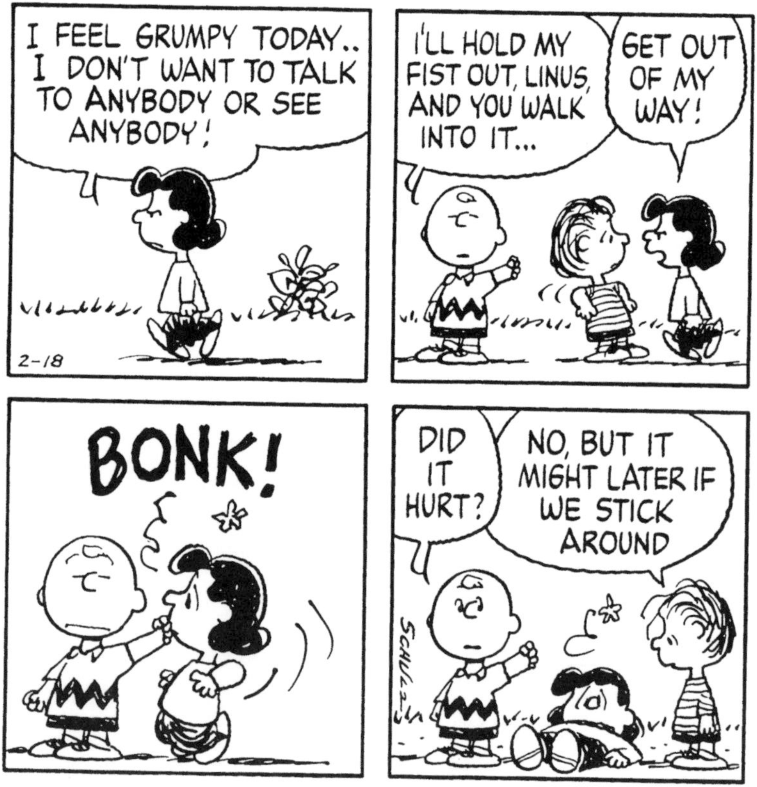
I FEEL GRUMPY TODAY.. I DON'T WANT TO TALK TO ANYBODY OR SEE ANYBODY!
2-18
I'LL HOLD MY FIST OUT, LINUS, AND YOU WALK INTO IT...
GET OUT OF MY WAY!
BONK!
DID IT HURT?
NO, BUT IT MIGHT LATER IF WE STICK AROUND
SCHULZ

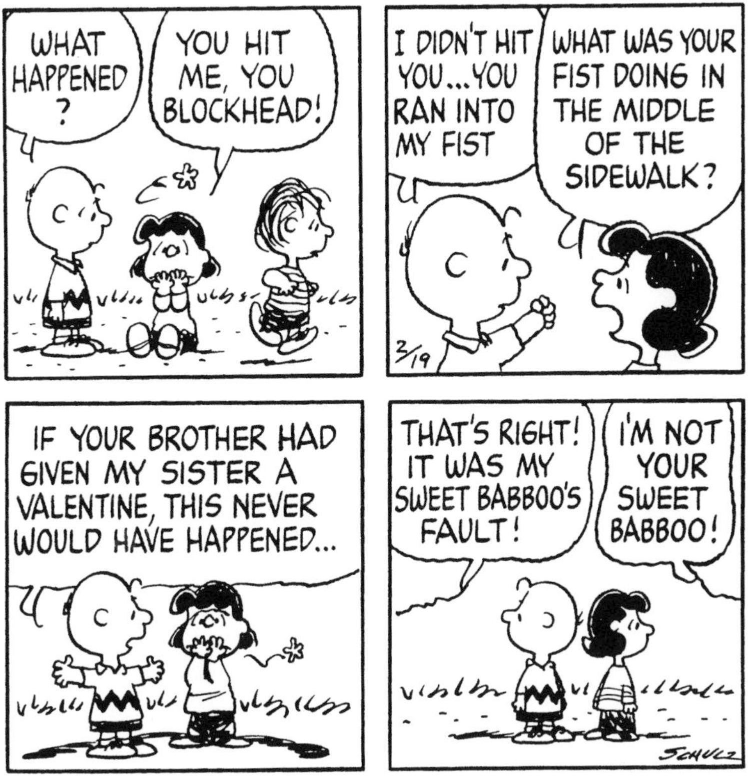
WHAT HAPPENED ?
YOU HIT ME, YOU BLOCKHEAD!
I DIDN'T HIT YOU...YOU RAN INTO MY FIST
WHAT WAS YOUR FIST DOING IN THE MIDDLE OF THE SIDEWALK?
2/19
IF YOUR BROTHER HAD GIVEN MY SISTER A VALENTINE, THIS NEVER WOULD HAVE HAPPENED...
THAT'S RIGHT! IT WAS MY SWEET BABBOO'S FAULT!
I'M NOT YOUR SWEET BABBOO!
SCHULZ

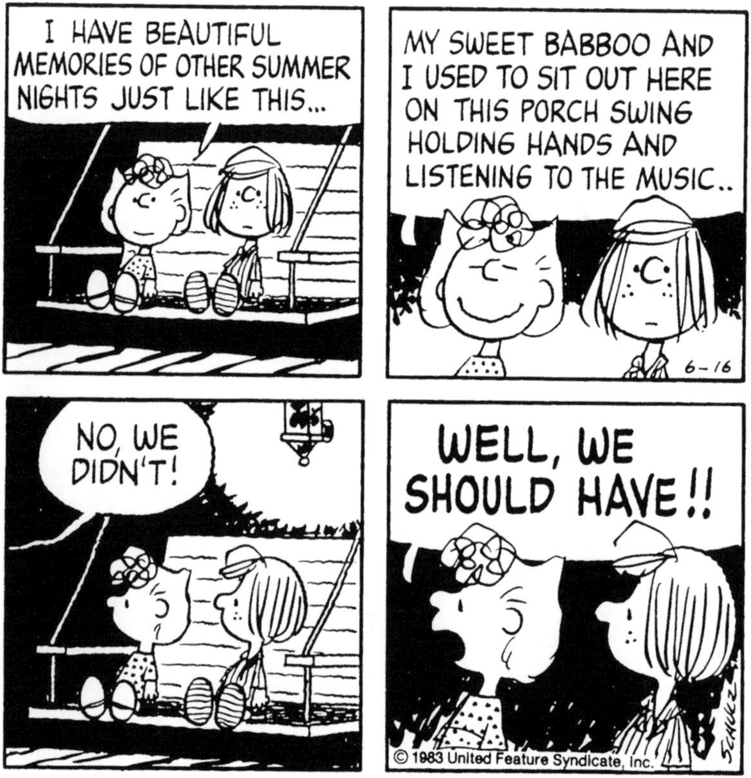
I HAVE BEAUTIFUL MEMORIES OF OTHER SUMMER NIGHTS JUST LIKE THIS...
MY SWEET BABBOO AND I USED TO SIT OUT HERE ON THIS PORCH SWING HOLDING HANDS AND LISTENING TO THE MUSIC..
6-16
NO, WE DIDN'T!
WELL, WE SHOULD HAVE!!
SCHULZ
© 1983 United Feature Syndicate, Inc.

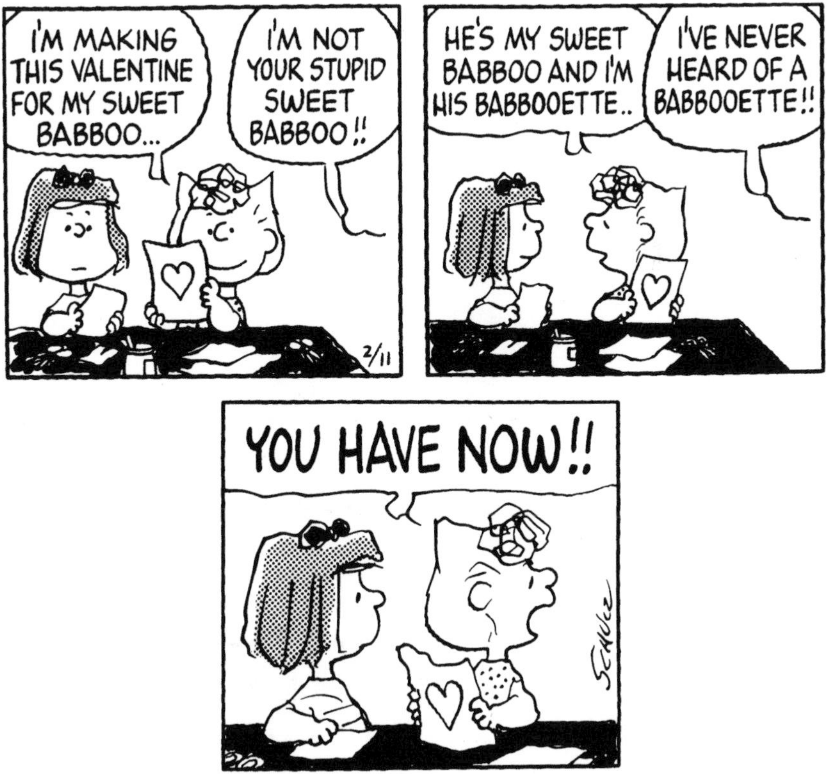
I'M MAKING THIS VALENTINE FOR MY SWEET BABBOO...
I'M NOT YOUR STUPID SWEET BABBOO!!
2/11
HE'S MY SWEET BABBOO AND I'M HIS BABBOOETTE..
I'VE NEVER HEARD OF A BABBOOETTE!!
YOU HAVE NOW!!
SCHULZ

A VALENTINE FOR CHARLIE BROWN
Charles M. Schulz

Editor: Gary Groth
Designer: Tony Ong
Associate Publisher: Eric Reynolds
Publisher: Gary Groth

A Valentine for Charlie Brown is copyright © 2015 Peanuts Worldwide,
LLC. All rights reserved. Permission to duplicate materials from
Peanuts comic strips must be obtained from Peanuts Worldwide.

Fantagraphics Books, 7563 Lake City Way NE, Seattle, WA 98115, USA.

For a free full-color catalog of comics, including *The Complete
Peanuts* and other assorted *Peanuts* books, call 1-800-657-1100. Our
books may be viewed and purchased on our website at
www.fantagraphics.com.

ISBN 978-1-60699-804-5   First printing: February 2015   Printed in China